W9-AMQ-401

At Issue

Embryonic and
Adult Stem Cells

Other Books in the At Issue Series:

At Issue

Embryonic and Adult Stem Cells

Susan Hunnicutt, Book Editor

GREENHAVEN PRESS
A part of Gale, Cengage Learning

Detroit • New York • San Francisco • New Haven, Conn • Waterville, Maine • London

GALE
CENGAGE Learning·

Elizabeth Des Chenes, *Director, Publishing Solutions*

© 2013 Greenhaven Press, a part of Gale, Cengage Learning

Gale and Greenhaven Press are registered trademarks used herein under license.

For more information, contact:
Greenhaven Press
27500 Drake Rd.
Farmington Hills, MI 48331-3535
Or you can visit our Internet site at gale.cengage.com

ALL RIGHTS RESERVED.
No part of this work covered by the copyright herein may be reproduced, transmitted, stored, or used in any form or by any means graphic, electronic, or mechanical, including but not limited to photocopying, recording, scanning, digitizing, taping, Web distribution, information networks, or information storage and retrieval systems, except as permitted under Section 107 or 108 of the 1976 United States Copyright Act, without the prior written permission of the publisher.

For product information and technology assistance, contact us at

Gale Customer Support, 1-800-877-4253
For permission to use material from this text or product, submit all requests online at
www.cengage.com/permissions

Further permissions questions can be emailed to permissionrequest@cengage.com

Articles in Greenhaven Press anthologies are often edited for length to meet page requirements. In addition, original titles of these works are changed to clearly present the main thesis and to explicitly indicate the author's opinion. Every effort is made to ensure that Greenhaven Press accurately reflects the original intent of the authors. Every effort has been made to trace the owners of copyrighted material.

Cover image © Images.com/Corbis.

LIBRARY OF CONGRESS CATALOGING-IN-PUBLICATION DATA

Embryonic and Adult Stem Cells / Susan Hunnicutt, book editor.
   p. cm. -- (At issue)
   Summary: "At Issue: Embryonic and Adult Stem Cells: Books in this anthology series focus a wide range of viewpoints onto a single controversial issue, providing in-depth discussions by leading advocates, a quick grounding in the issues, and a challenge to critical thinking skills"-- Provided by publisher.
   Includes bibliographical references and index.
   ISBN 978-0-7377-6173-3 (hardback) -- ISBN 978-0-7377-6174-0 (paperback)
   1. Stem cells. 2. Embryonic stem cells. I. Hunnicutt, Susan.
   QH588.S83E453 2013
   616.02'774--dc23
                                      2012039340

Printed in the United States of America
1 2 3 4 5   17 16 15 14 13

Contents

Introduction

Stem cells play critical roles in the development of complex organisms. Embryonic stem cells have the ability to differentiate, giving rise to the many other types of cells and tissues that make up healthy, fully developed bodies. Then, as organisms age, another group of stem cells known as "somatic" or "adult" stem cells are key to the repair and replenishment of some tissues, such as the colon and bone marrow.

The ability of stem cells to renew themselves through cell division, sometimes after long periods of inactivity, and their ability under certain conditions to develop from an unspecialized state into tissue- or organ-specific cells are the two characteristics that distinguish stem cells from other types of cells. Because of their powerful generative properties, both embryonic and somatic stem cells have become an important focus of current biomedical research. Scientists have studied embryonic stem cells to learn more about normal processes of prenatal growth and development. And many scientists studying both embryonic and adult stem cells hope one day to be able to apply what they learn to develop new organs and tissues that can replace others that have been destroyed or damaged by accident or disease. Osteoarthritis and rheumatoid arthritis, spinal cord injuries, strokes, burns, heart disease, diabetes, and Alzheimer's disease are some of the conditions for which stem cell treatments are envisioned. Researchers have also developed stem cell cultures that can be used to test new drug therapies.

While both embryonic and adult stem cells hold out the promise of new treatments for disease, studies involving human embryonic stem cells have proven controversial. Research on embryonic stem cells requires the destruction of human embryos. Some have argued that for ethical reasons research should be confined to adult or somatic stems cells, and that research involving embryonic cells should be halted.

Now, in a new development more focused on the role of adult or somatic stem cells in causing disease, some researchers are proposing that stem cells may be responsible for the abnormal growth of cancer cells.

In the conventional view, cancer is seen as starting with the division of a single mutated cell and progressing in a manner that has been described as "equal opportunity": all cancerous cells comprising a tumor have roughly the same ability to divide and contribute to the further growth of the tumor. Assuming this to be the case, anti-cancer therapies up to now have been developed to concentrate on reducing tumor size. The assumption has been that all tumor cells need to be eliminated in order to halt the growth of cancer. But three studies published in August 2012 have focused attention on the idea that tumors contain small populations of cancer-initiating stem cells that fuel abnormal growth, while other tumor cells actually contribute little to the growth of the cancer.

In one study, a group of researchers at Southwestern Medical Center in Dallas, Texas, were looking at a lethal form of brain cancer in genetically engineered mice. Chemotherapy was used to stop the growth of the tumors, but once therapy stopped, the abnormal growth resumed. Molecular analysis of the reemergent cancerous tissues showed that a small number of stem cells within the tumor had begun to divide, and were the source of the new tumor cells. According to Luis Parada, the head of the research team, the findings show that cancer treatments should focus on eliminating the cancer-inducing stem cells, rather than simply on reducing the overall size of the tumor.

A second study, conducted in the Netherlands, studied stem cell-like properties in intestinal cancers of mice, while a third conducted in Brussels, Belgium, looked at squamous cell skin cancers. These studies also found that tumor growth appeared to be fueled by cancer-initiating stem cells.

If the theory proves to be true, the discovery may lead to new ways to prevent or cure cancer. But not all scientists are persuaded. Scott Kern, who studies cancer at Johns Hopkins University in Baltimore, Maryland, believes the results of the study conducted at Southwestern Medical Center can be explained without relying on the cancer stem cell theory. He points out that the two studies conducted in Europe were focused on lesions that can lead to tumors. Because all three studies were conducted in mice rather than in human subjects, he questions whether any of the findings can be generalized to include human populations.

Researchers have learned a great deal about the role of stem cells in the development of healthy organisms. Yet much remains to be learned, both about the potential of stem cells to heal and restore damaged tissue and about the possible role stem cells may play in the development of diseases like cancer. Should scientific research be limited to adult or somatic stem cells, or is it important for inquiry involving embryonic stem cells to continue as well? What unique ethical challenges are emerging from research involving adult stem cells? Should practicing physicians be permitted to offer experimental stem cell therapies before their effectiveness has been proven in clinical trials? What role should the government play in regulating the therapeutic uses of stem cells? These are some of the questions that are explored in *At Issue: Embryonic and Adult Stem Cells*.

1

Stem Cells: An Overview

National Institutes of Health

The National Institutes of Health (NIH) is part of the US Department of Health and Human Services. It is the medical research agency of the US government and the largest source of funding for medical research in the world.

Stem cells are cells that have the ability to develop into many different cell types in the body during early life and growth. In addition, in many tissues they serve as a sort of internal repair system, dividing without limit to replenish other cells. Scientists believe that because of their regenerative abilities, stem cells offer promise for treating diseases such as diabetes and heart disease.

Stem cells differ from other kinds of cells in the body. All stem cells—regardless of their source—have three general properties: they are capable of dividing and renewing themselves for long periods; they are unspecialized; and they can give rise to specialized cell types.

What Are the Unique Properties of All Stem Cells?

Stem cells are capable of dividing and renewing themselves for long periods. Unlike muscle cells, blood cells, or nerve cells—which do not normally replicate themselves—stem cells may replicate many times, or proliferate. A starting population of stem cells that proliferates for many months in the laboratory

"Stem Cell Basics," National Institutes of Health, US Department of Health and Human Services, 2009.

can yield millions of cells. If the resulting cells continue to be unspecialized, like the parent stem cells, the cells are said to be capable of long-term self-renewal.

The specific factors and conditions that allow stem cells to remain unspecialized are of great interest to scientists.

Scientists are trying to understand two fundamental properties of stem cells that relate to their long-term self-renewal:

1. why can embryonic stem cells proliferate for a year or more in the laboratory without differentiating, but most non-embryonic stem cells cannot; and

2. what are the factors in living organisms that normally regulate stem cell proliferation and self-renewal?

Discovering the answers to these questions may make it possible to understand how cell proliferation is regulated during normal embryonic development or during the abnormal cell division that leads to cancer. Such information would also enable scientists to grow embryonic and non-embryonic stem cells more efficiently in the laboratory.

The specific factors and conditions that allow stem cells to remain unspecialized are of great interest to scientists. It has taken scientists many years of trial and error to learn to derive and maintain stem cells in the laboratory without them spontaneously differentiating into specific cell types. For example, it took two decades to learn how to grow human embryonic stem cells in the laboratory following the development of conditions for growing mouse stem cells. Therefore, understanding the signals in a mature organism that cause a stem cell population to proliferate and remain unspecialized until the cells are needed. Such information is critical for scientists to be able to grow large numbers of unspecialized stem cells in the laboratory for further experimentation.

Stem cells are unspecialized. One of the fundamental properties of a stem cell is that it does not have any tissue-specific structures that allow it to perform specialized functions. For example, a stem cell cannot work with its neighbors to pump blood through the body (like a heart muscle cell), and it cannot carry oxygen molecules through the bloodstream (like a red blood cell). However, unspecialized stem cells can give rise to specialized cells, including heart muscle cells, blood cells, or nerve cells.

Stem cells can give rise to specialized cells. When unspecialized stem cells give rise to specialized cells, the process is called differentiation. While differentiating, the cell usually goes through several stages, becoming more specialized at each step. Scientists are just beginning to understand the signals inside and outside cells that trigger each stem of the differentiation process. The internal signals are controlled by a cell's genes, which are interspersed across long strands of DNA, and carry coded instructions for all cellular structures and functions. The external signals for cell differentiation include chemicals secreted by other cells, physical contact with neighboring cells, and certain molecules in the microenvironment. The interaction of signals during differentiation causes the cell's DNA to acquire epigenetic marks that restrict DNA expression in the cell and can be passed on through cell division.

Many questions about stem cell differentiation remain. For example, are the internal and external signals for cell differentiation similar for all kinds of stem cells? Can specific sets of signals be identified that promote differentiation into specific cell types? Addressing these questions may lead scientists to find new ways to control stem cell differentiation in the laboratory, thereby growing cells or tissues that can be used for specific purposes such as cell-based therapies or drug screening.

Adult stem cells typically generate the cell types of the tissue in which they reside. For example, a blood-forming adult stem cell in the bone marrow normally gives rise to the many types of blood cells. It is generally accepted that a blood-forming cell in the bone marrow—which is called a hematopoietic stem cell—cannot give rise to the cells of a very different tissue, such as nerve cells in the brain. Experiments over the last several years have purported to show that stem cells from one tissue may give rise to cell types of a completely different tissue. This remains an area of great debate within the research community. This controversy demonstrates the challenges of studying adult stem cells and suggests that additional research using adult stem cells is necessary to understand their full potential as future therapies.

What Are Embryonic Stem Cells?

What stages of early embryonic development are important for generating embryonic stem cells?

Embryonic stem cells, as their name suggests, are derived from embryos. Most embryonic stem cells are derived from embryos that develop from eggs that have been fertilized *in vitro*—in an *in vitro* fertilization clinic—and then donated for research purposes with informed consent of the donors. They are *not* derived from eggs fertilized in a woman's body.

Once the cell line is established, the original cells yield millions of embryonic stem cells.

How are embryonic stem cells grown in the laboratory?

Growing cells in the laboratory is known as cell culture. Human embryonic stem cells (hESCs) are generated by transferring cells from a preimplantation-stage embryo into a plastic laboratory culture dish that contains a nutrient broth known as culture medium. The cells divide and spread over the surface of the dish. The inner surface of the culture dish is typically coated with mouse embryonic skin cells that have been treated so they will not divide. This coating layer of cells is called a feeder layer. The mouse cells in the bottom of the culture dish provide the cells a sticky surface to which they can attach. Also, the feeder cells release nutrients into the culture medium. Researchers have devised ways to grow embryonic stem cells without mouse feeder cells. This is a significant scientific advance because of the risk that viruses or other macromolecules in the mouse cells may be transmitted to the human cells.

The process of generating an embryonic stem cell line is somewhat inefficient, so lines are not produced each time cells from the preimplantation-stage embryo are placed into a culture dish. However, if the plated cells survive, divide and multiply enough to crowd the dish, they are removed gently and plated into several fresh culture dishes. The process of replating or subculturing the cells is repeated many times and for many months. Each cycle of subculturing the cells is referred to as a passage. Once the cell line is established, the original cells yield millions of embryonic stem cells. Embryonic stem cells that have proliferated in cell culture for a prolonged period of time without differentiating, are pluripotent, and have not developed genetic abnormalities are referred to as an embryonic stem cell line. At any stage in the process, batches of cells can be frozen and shipped to other laboratories for further culture and experimentation. . . .

If scientists can reliably direct the differentiation of embryonic stem cells into specific cell types, they may be able to use the resulting, differentiated cells to treat certain diseases in the future.

As long as the embryonic stem cells in culture are grown under appropriate conditions, they can remain undifferentiated (unspecialized). But if cells are allowed to clump together to form embryoid bodies, they begin to differentiate spontaneously. They can form muscle cells, nerve cells, and many other cell types. Although spontaneous differentiation is a good indication that a culture of embryonic stem cells is healthy, it is not an efficient way to produce cultures of specific cell types.

So, to generate cultures of specific types of differentiated cells—heart muscle cells, blood cells, or nerve cells, for example—scientists try to control the differentiation of embryonic stem cells. They change the chemical composition of the culture medium, alter the surface of the culture dish, or modify the cells by inserting specific genes. Through years of experimentation, scientists have established some basic protocols or "recipes" for the directed differentiation of embryonic stem cells into some specific cell types.

If scientists can reliably direct the differentiation of embryonic stem cells into specific cell types, they may be able to use the resulting, differentiated cells to treat certain diseases in the future. Diseases that might be treated by transplanting cells generated from human embryonic stem cells include Parkinson's disease, diabetes, traumatic spinal cord injury, Duchenne's muscular dystrophy, heart disease, and vision and hearing loss.

Adult stem cells have been identified in many organs and tissues, including brain, bone marrow, peripheral blood, blood vessels, skeletal muscle, skin, teeth, heart, gut, liver, ovarian epithelium, and testis.

What Are Adult Stem Cells?

An adult stem cell is thought to be an undifferentiated cell, found among differentiated cells in a tissue or organ that can renew itself and can differentiate to yield some or all of the major specialized cell types of the tissue or organ. The primary roles of adult stem cells in a living organism are to maintain and repair the tissue in which they are found. Scientists also use the term somatic stem cell instead of adult stem cell, where somatic refers to cells of the body (not the germ cells, sperm or eggs). Unlike embryonic stem cells, which are defined by their origin (cells from the preimplantation-stage embryo), the origin of adult stem cells in some mature tissues is still under investigation.

Research on adult stem cells has generated a great deal of excitement. Scientists have found adult stem cells in many more tissues than they once thought possible. This finding has led researchers and clinicians to ask whether adult stem cells could be used for transplants. In fact, adult hematopoietic, or blood-forming, stem cells from bone marrow have been used in transplants for 40 years. Scientists now have evidence that stem cells exist in the brain and the heart. If the differentiation of adult stem cells can be controlled in the laboratory, these cells may become the basis of transplantation-based therapies. . . .

Where are adult stem cells found, and what do they normally do?

Adult stem cells have been identified in many organs and tissues, including brain, bone marrow, peripheral blood, blood vessels, skeletal muscle, skin, teeth, heart, gut, liver, ovarian epithelium, and testis. They are thought to reside in a specific area of each tissue (called a "stem cell niche"). In many tissues, current evidence suggests that some types of stem cells are pericytes, cells that compose the outermost layer of small blood vessels. Stem cells may remain quiescent (non-dividing) for long periods of time until they are activated by a normal need for more cells to maintain tissues, or by disease or tissue injury.

Typically, there is a very small number of stem cells in each tissue, and once removed from the body, their capacity to divide is limited, making generation of large quantities of stem cells difficult. Scientists in many laboratories are trying to find better ways to grow large quantities of adult stem cells in cell culture and to manipulate them to generate specific cell types so they can be used to treat injury or disease. Some examples of potential treatments include regenerating bone using cells derived from bone marrow stroma, developing insulin-producing cells for type 1 diabetes, and repairing damaged heart muscle following a heart attack with cardiac muscle cells. . . .

As indicated above, scientists have reported that adult stem cells occur in many tissues and that they enter normal differentiation pathways to form the specialized cell types of the tissue in which they reside.

Normal differentiation pathways of adult stem cells. In a living animal, adult stem cells are available to divide, when needed, and can give rise to mature cell types that have characteristic shapes and specialized structures and functions of a particular tissue. The following are examples of differentiation pathways of adult stem cells that have been demonstrated *in vitro* or *in vivo*.

Hematopoietic stem cells give rise to all the types of blood cells: red blood cells, B lymphocytes, T lymphocytes, natural killer cells, neutrophils, basophils, eosinophils, monocytes, and macrophages.

Mesenchymal stem cells give rise to a variety of cell types: bone cells (osteocytes), cartilage cells (chondrocytes), fat cells (adipocytes), and other kinds of connective tissue cells such as those in tendons.

Neural stem cells in the brain give rise to its three major cell types: nerve cells (neurons) and two categories of non-neuronal cells—astrocytes and oligodendrocytes.

Epithelial stem cells in the lining of the digestive tract occur in deep crypts and give rise to several cell types: absorptive cells, goblet cells, paneth cells, and enteroendocrine cells.

Skin stem cells occur in the basal layer of the epidermis and at the base of hair follicles. The epidermal stem cells give rise to keratinocytes, which migrate to the surface of the skin and form a protective layer. The follicular stem cells can give rise to both the hair follicle and to the epidermis.

Transdifferentiation. A number of experiments have reported that certain adult stem cell types can differentiate into cell types seen in organs or tissues other than those expected from the cells' predicted lineage (i.e., brain stem cells that differentiate into blood cells or blood-forming cells that differentiate into cardiac muscle cells, and so forth). This reported phenomenon is called transdifferentiation.

Induced pluripotent stem cells (iPSCs) are adult cells that have been genetically reprogrammed to an embryonic stem cell-like state.

Although isolated instances of transdifferentiation have been observed in some vertebrate species, whether this phenomenon actually occurs in humans is under debate by the scientific community. Instead of transdifferentiation, the observed instances may involve fusion of a donor cell with a recipient cell. Another possibility is that transplanted stem cells are secreting factors that encourage the recipient's own stem cells to begin the repair process. Even when transdifferentiation has been detected, only a very small percentage of cells undergo the process.

In a variation of transdifferentiation experiments, scientists have recently demonstrated that certain adult cell types can be "reprogrammed" into other cell types in vivo using a well-controlled process of genetic modification. This strategy may offer a way to reprogram available cells into other cell types that have been lost or damaged due to disease. For example, one recent experiment shows how pancreatic beta cells, the insulin-producing cells that are lost or damaged in diabetes, could possibly be created by reprogramming other pancreatic cells. By "re-starting" expression of three critical beta-cell genes in differentiated adult pancreatic exocrine cells, researchers were able to create beta cell-like cells that can secrete insulin. The reprogrammed cells were similar to beta cells in appearance, size, and shape; expressed genes characteristic of beta cells; and were able to partially restore blood sugar regulation in mice whose own beta cells had been chemically destroyed. While not transdifferentiation by definition, this method for reprogramming adult cells may be used as a model for directly reprogramming other adult cell types.

In addition to reprogramming cells to become a specific cell type, it is now possible to reprogram adult somatic cells to become like embryonic stem cells (induced pluripotent stem cells, iPSCs) through the introduction of embryonic genes. Thus, a source of cells can be generated that are specific to the donor, thereby increasing the chance of compatibility if such cells were to be used for tissue regeneration. However, like embryonic stem cells, determination of the methods by which iPSCs can be completely and reproducibly committed to appropriate cell lineages is still under investigation. . . .

Some of the most serious medical conditions, such as cancer and birth defects, are due to abnormal cell division and differentiation.

What Are Induced Pluripotent Stem Cells?

Induced pluripotent stem cells (iPSCs) are adult cells that have been genetically reprogrammed to an embryonic stem cell-like state by being forced to express genes and factors important for maintaining the defining properties of embryonic stem cells. Although these cells meet the defining criteria for pluripotent stem cells, it is not known if iPSCs and embryonic stem cells differ in clinically significant ways. Mouse iPSCs were first reported in 2006, and human iPSCs were first reported in late 2007. Mouse iPSCs demonstrate important characteristics of pluripotent stem cells, including expressing stem cell markers, forming tumors containing cells from all three germ layers, and being able to contribute to many different tissues when injected into mouse embryos at a very early stage in development. Human iPSCs also express stem cell markers and are capable of generating cells characteristic of all three germ layers.

Although additional research is needed, iPSCs are already useful tools for drug development and modeling of diseases, and scientists hope to use them in transplantation medicine. Viruses are currently used to introduce the reprogramming factors into adult cells, and this process must be carefully controlled and tested before the technique can lead to useful treatments for humans. In animal studies, the virus used to introduce the stem cell factors sometimes causes cancers. Researchers are currently investigating non-viral delivery strategies. In any case, this breakthrough discovery has created a powerful new way to "de-differentiate" cells whose developmental fates had been previously assumed to be determined. In addition, tissues derived from iPSCs will be a nearly identical match to the cell donor and thus probably avoid rejection by the immune system. The iPSC strategy creates pluripotent stem cells that, together with studies of other types of pluripotent stem cells, will help researchers learn how to reprogram cells to repair damaged tissues in the human body.

What Are the Potential Uses of Human Stem Cells and Obstacles That Must Be Overcome?

There are many ways in which human stem cells can be used in research and the clinic. Studies of human embryonic stem cells will yield information about the complex events that occur during human development. A primary goal of this work is to identify how undifferentiated stem cells become the differentiated cells that form the tissues and organs. Scientists know that turning genes on and off is central to this process. Some of the most serious medical conditions, such as cancer and birth defects, are due to abnormal cell division and differentiation. A more complete understanding of the genetic and molecular controls of these processes may yield information about how such diseases arise and suggest new strategies for therapy. Predictably controlling cell proliferation and differentiation requires additional basic research on the molecular and genetic signals that regulate cell division and specialization. While recent developments with iPS cells suggest some of the specific factors that may be involved, techniques must be devised to introduce these factors safely into the cells and control the processes that are induced by these factors.

Human stem cells could also be used to test new drugs. For example, new medications could be tested for safety on differentiated cells generated from human pluripotent cell lines. Other kinds of cell lines are already used in this way. Cancer cell lines, for example, are used to screen potential anti-tumor drugs. The availability of pluripotent stem cells would allow drug testing in a wider range of cell types. However, to screen drugs effectively, the conditions must be identical when comparing different drugs. Therefore, scientists will have to be able to precisely control the differentiation of stem cells into the specific cell type on which drugs will be tested. Current knowledge of the signals controlling differentiation falls short of being able to mimic these conditions precisely to generate pure populations of differentiated cells for each drug being tested.

Perhaps the most important potential application of human stem cells is the generation of cells and tissues that could be used for cell-based therapies. Today, donated organs and tissues are often used to replace ailing or destroyed tissue, but the need for transplantable tissues and organs far outweighs the available supply. Stem cells, directed to differentiate into specific cell types, offer the possibility of a renewable source of replacement cells and tissues to treat diseases including Alzheimer's diseases, spinal cord injury, stroke, burns, heart disease, diabetes, osteoarthritis, and rheumatoid arthritis.

For example, it may become possible to generate healthy heart muscle cells in the laboratory and then transplant those cells into patients with chronic heart disease. Preliminary research in mice and other animals indicates that bone marrow stromal cells, transplanted into a damaged heart, can have beneficial effects. Whether these cells can generate heart muscle cells or stimulate the growth of new blood vessels that repopulate the heart tissue, or help via some other mechanism is actively under investigation. For example, injected cells may accomplish repair by secreting growth factors, rather than actually incorporating into the heart. Promising results from animal studies have served as the basis for a small number of exploratory studies in humans. Other recent studies in cell culture systems indicate that it may be possible to direct the differentiation of embryonic stem cells or adult bone marrow cells into heart muscle cells. . . .

In people who suffer from type 1 diabetes, the cells of the pancreas that normally produce insulin are destroyed by the patient's own immune system. New studies indicate that it may be possible to direct the differentiation of human embryonic stem cells in cell culture to form insulin-producing cells that eventually could be used in transplantation therapy for persons with diabetes. . . .

To realize the promise of novel cell-based therapies for such pervasive and debilitating diseases, scientists must be able to manipulate stem cells so that they possess the necessary characteristics for successful differentiation, transplantation, and engraftment. The following is a list of steps in successful cell-based treatments that scientists will have to learn to control to bring such treatments to the clinic. To be useful for transplant purposes, stem cells must be reproducibly made to:

- Proliferate extensively and generate sufficient quantities of tissue.

- Differentiate into the desired cell type(s).

- Survive in the recipient after transplant.

- Integrate into the surrounding tissue after transplant.

- Function appropriately for the duration of the recipient's life.

- Avoid harming the recipient in any way.

Also, to avoid the problem of immune rejection, scientists are experimenting with different research strategies to generate tissues that will not be rejected.

To summarize, stem cells offer exciting promise for future therapies, but significant technical hurdles remain that will only be overcome through years of intensive research.

2

Research Is Needed to Prove the Effectiveness of Various Stem Cell Therapies

International Society for Stem Cell Research

The International Society for Stem Cell Research (ISSCR) is an independent, nonprofit organization established to promote the exchange of information about stem cells, to educate the public, and to encourage research and the application of knowledge arising from research about stem cells.

A great deal of misinformation is being circulated about what stem cells are and what is possible with stem cell therapies. Stem cell science is promising but in many areas more research will be necessary in order to develop safe and effective treatments.

Many clinics that are offering stem cell treatments make claims about what stem cells can and cannot do that are not supported by our understanding of science. . . .

1. There Are Different Types of Stem Cells—Each with Their Own Purpose

There are many different types of stem cells that come from different places in the body or are formed at different times in our lives. These include embryonic stem cells that exist only at the earliest stages of development and various types of 'tissue-

"Top Ten Things to Know About Stem Cell Treatments," International Society for Stem Cell Research, www.closerlookatstemcells.org; accessed December 6, 2012. Copyright © by ISSCR. All rights reserved. Reproduced by permission.

specific' or 'adult' stem cells that appear during fetal development and remain in our bodies throughout life.

Our bodies use different types of tissue-specific stem cells to fit a particular purpose. Tissue-specific stem cells are limited in their potential and largely make the cell types found in the tissue from which they are derived. For example, the blood-forming stem cells (or hematopoietic stem cells) in the bone marrow regenerate the blood, while neural stem cells in the brain make brain cells. A neural stem cell won't spontaneously make a blood cell and likewise a hematopoietic stem cell won't spontaneously make a brain cell. Thus, it is unlikely that a single cell type could be used to treat a multitude of unrelated diseases that involve different tissues or organs. *Be wary of clinics that offer treatments with stem cells that originate from a part of the body that is different from the part being treated.*

The range of diseases where stem cell treatments have been shown to be beneficial in responsibly conducted clinical trials is still extremely restricted.

---

2. A Single Stem Cell Treatment Will Not Work on a Multitude of Unrelated Diseases or Conditions

As described above, each type of stem cell fulfills a specific function in the body and cannot be expected to make cell types from other tissues. Thus, it is unlikely that a single type of stem cell treatment can treat multiple unrelated conditions, such as diabetes and Parkinson's disease. The underlying causes are very different and different cell types would need to be replaced to treat each condition. It is critical that the cell type used as a treatment be appropriate to the specific disease or condition.

Embryonic stem cells may one day be used to generate treatments for a range of human diseases. However, embryonic stem cells themselves cannot directly be used for therapies as they would likely cause tumors and are unlikely to become the cells needed to regenerate a tissue on their own. They would first need to be coaxed to develop into specialized cell types before transplantation. *A major warning sign that a clinic may not be credible is when treatments are offered for a wide variety of conditions but rely on a single cell type.*

3. Currently There Are Very Few Widely Accepted Stem Cell Therapies

The range of diseases where stem cell treatments have been shown to be beneficial in responsibly conducted clinical trials is still extremely restricted. The best defined and most extensively used is blood stem cell transplantation to treat diseases and conditions of the blood and immune system, or to restore the blood system after treatments for specific cancers. Some bone, skin and corneal diseases or injuries can be treated with grafting of tissue that depends upon stem cells from these organs. These therapies are also generally accepted as safe and effective by the medical community.

4. Just Because People Say Stem Cells Helped Them Doesn't Mean They Did

There are three main reasons why a person might feel better that are unrelated to the actual stem cell treatment: the 'placebo effect', accompanying treatments, and natural fluctuations of the disease or condition. The intense desire or belief that a treatment will work can cause a person to feel like it has and to even experience positive physical changes, such as improved movement or less pain. This phenomenon is called the placebo effect. Even having a positive conversation with a doctor can cause a person to feel improvement. Likewise, other techniques offered along with stem cell treatment—such as changes to diet, relaxation, physical therapy, medication, etc.—may make a person feel better in a way that is unrelated to the stem cells. Also, the severity of symptoms of many conditions can change over time, resulting in either temporary improvement or decline, which can complicate the interpretation of the effectiveness of treatments. These factors are so widespread that without testing in a controlled clinical study, where a group that receives a treatment is carefully compared against a group that does not receive this treatment, it is very difficult to determine the real effect of any therapy. *Be wary of clinics that measure or advertise their results primarily through patient testimonials.*

The procedure to either remove or inject [stem cells] . . . carries risk, from introducing an infection to damaging the tissue into which they are injected.

---

5. A Large Part of Why It Takes Time to Develop New Therapies Is That Science Itself Is a Long and Difficult Process

Science, in general, is a long and involved process. Understanding what goes wrong in disease or injury and how to fix it takes time. New ideas have to be tested first in a research laboratory, and many times the new ideas don't work. Even once the basic science has been established, translating it into an effective medical treatment is a long and difficult process. Something that looks promising in cultured cells may fail as a therapy in an animal model and something that works in an animal model may fail when it is tried on humans. Once therapies are tested in humans, ensuring patient safety becomes a critical issue and this means starting with very few people until the safety and side effects are better understood.

If a treatment has not been carefully designed, well studied and gone through the necessary preclinical and clinical testing, it is unlikely to have the desired effect. Even more concerning is that it may prove to make the condition worse or have dangerous side effects.

6. To Be Used in Treatments, Stem Cells Will Have to Be Instructed to Behave in Specific Ways

Bone marrow transplantation is typically successful because we are asking the cells to do exactly what they were designed to do, make more blood. For other conditions, we may want the cells to behave in ways that are different from how they would ordinarily work in the body. One of the greatest barriers to the development of successful stem cell therapies is to get the cells to behave in the desired way. Also, once transplanted inside the body the cells need to integrate and function in concert with the body's other cells. For example, to treat many neurological conditions the cells we implant will need to grow into specific types of neurons, and to work they will also have to know which other neurons to make connections with and how to make these connections. We are still learning about how to direct stem cells to become the right cell type, to grow only as much as we need them to, and the best ways to transplant them. Discovering how to do all this will take time. *Be wary of claims that stem cells will somehow just know where to go and what to do to treat a specific condition.*

7. Just Because Stem Cells Came from Your Body Doesn't Mean They Are Safe

Every medical procedure has risks. While you are unlikely to have an immune response to your own cells, the procedures used to acquire, grow and deliver them are potentially risky. As soon as the cells leave your body they may be subjected to a number of manipulations that could change the characteristics of the cells. If they are grown in culture (a process called expansion), the cells may lose the normal mechanisms that control growth or may lose the ability to specialize into the cell types you need. The cells may become contaminated with bacteria, viruses or other pathogens that could cause disease. The procedure to either remove or inject the cells also carries risk, from introducing an infection to damaging the tissue into which they are injected.

8. There Is Something to Lose By Trying an Unproven Treatment

Some of the conditions that clinics claim are treatable with stem cells are considered incurable by other means. It is easy to understand why people might feel they have nothing to lose from trying something even if it is unproven. However, there are very real risks of developing complications, both immediate and long-term, while the chance of experiencing a benefit is likely very low. In one publicized case, a young boy developed brain tumors as a result of a stem cell treatment. Participating in an unproven treatment may make a person ineligible to participate in upcoming clinical trials (see also number 9). Where cost is high, there may be long-term financial implications for patients, their families and communities. If travel is involved there are additional considerations, not the least of which is being away from family and friends.

9. An Experimental Treatment Offered for Sale Is Not the Same as a Clinical Trial

The fact that a procedure is experimental does not automatically mean that it is part of a research study or clinical trial. A responsible clinical trial can be characterized by a number of key features. There is preclinical data supporting that the treatment being tested is likely to be safe and effective. Before starting, there is oversight by an independent group such as an Institutional Review Board or medical ethics committee that protect patients' rights, and in many countries the trial is assessed and approved by a national regulatory agency, such as the European Medicines Agency (EMA) or the U.S. Food and Drug Administration (FDA). The study itself is designed to answer specific questions about a new treatment or a new way of using current treatments, often with a control group to which the group of people receiving the new treatment is compared. Typically, the cost of the new treatment and trial monitoring is defrayed by the company developing the treatment or by local or national government funding. *Beware of expensive treatments that have not passed successfully through clinical trials.*

Responsibly-conducted clinical trials are critical to the development of new treatments as they allow us to learn whether these treatments are safe and effective. The ISSCR supports participation in responsible clinical trials after careful consideration of the issues highlighted on this site and in discussion with a trusted physician.

10. Stem Cell Science Is Constantly Moving Forward

Stem cell science is extraordinarily promising. There have been great advances in treating diseases and conditions of the blood system using blood-forming stem cells, and these show us just how powerful stem cell therapies can be. Scientists all over the world are researching ways to harness stem cells and use them to learn more about, to diagnose, and to treat various diseases and conditions. Every day scientists are working on new ways to shape and control different types of stem cells in ways that are bringing us closer to developing new treatments. Many potential treatments are currently being tested in animal models and some have already been brought to clinical trials. In February 2010 the British company ReNeuron announced it had been approved to conduct a Phase I clinical trial of a neural stem cell treatment for stroke. The first embryonic stem cell-based treatment for acute spinal cord injury has been authorized by the U.S. Food and Drug Administration (FDA) to move into Phase I clinical trials. Although it is sometimes hard to see, stem cell science is moving forward. We are tremendously optimistic that stem cell therapies will someday be available to treat a wide range of human diseases and conditions.

3

Adult Stem Cells Are More Beneficial than Embryonic Stem Cells

David A. Prentice

David A. Prentice is senior fellow for life sciences at the Family Research Council.

Advocates of embryonic stem cell research have begun to admit that embryonic stem cells have not delivered on their promise. Recently a California company, the first to receive approval to inject embryonic stem cells into humans, ended a clinical trial and shut down its stem cell research programs after patients showed no improvement in their conditions. Adult stem cells remain the only type of stem cells that have proven therapeutic benefits. Each year, over fifty thousand people are treated using adult stem cells.

Still confused by the stem cell debate? Don't feel alone. Medical professionals and the public alike still have many questions about the different types, or sources, of stem cells as well as their potential and actual effectiveness for clinical treatments.

Key Advocates Are Admitting Failure

Embryonic stem cells continue to receive the majority of news coverage, yet remain the least likely stem cell to help patients. In fact, even the embryonic stem cell advocates are beginning

David A. Prentice, "Adult Stem Cell Treatments Move Ahead, Embryonic Stem Cells Fall Farther Behind," National Right to Life News Today, May 24, 2012. Copyright © 2012 by National Right to Life Committee. All rights reserved. Reproduced by permission.

to admit failure. The California company Geron, first to receive approval to inject embryonic stem cells into a few patients, gave up on their trial and shut down all of their embryonic stem cell research. After a year, none of the patients showed improvements, though they will need to be monitored for many years to come for potential tumor formation. Even celebrity stem cell promoter Michael J. Fox recently admitted that "[embryonic] stem cells" were unlikely to help any patients any time soon.

Adult stem cells remain the only type of stem cell used successfully to treat human patients.

Given that embryonic stem cells are ethically tainted, requiring the destruction of young human life or even creating a new human life via cloning (somatic cell nuclear transfer) specifically for destruction, it's heartening that many are seeing the many problems associated with this type of stem cell.

The newer technology of iPS cells (induced pluripotent stem cells) has been increasingly in the news lately, as an ethical alternative to embryonic stem cells. The iPS cells are made by adding a few genes to a normal cell such as a skin cell, causing the normal cell to look and act like an embryonic stem cell, yet without any use of embryos, eggs, or cloning technology. Even though iPS cells use an adult cell (not a stem cell) as their starting material, they are definitely not "adult stem cells," but rather an ethically-derived version of embryonic stem cells. They can be made from any person, starting with almost any normal cell, and have been used to model cell growth and development in the lab. They may also serve as disease models in the lab, allowing scientists to investigate how some diseases develop. Recently, Israeli scientists made iPS cells from heart patients, then turned the iPS cells into beating heart cells in the lab, to study heart disease.

Adult Stem Cells Have Become the Gold Standard

Adult stem cells remain the only type of stem cell used successfully to treat human patients. They are the one and only gold standard for clinical treatments with stem cells. Adult stem cells have many advantages. They can be isolated from numerous tissues, including bone marrow, muscle, fat, and umbilical cord blood, just to name a few. And isolating the adult stem cells from tissues of a patient or a healthy donor does not require harming or destroying the donor, giving adult stem cells a decided ethical advantage over embryonic stem cells. Adult stem cells also have a proven track record for success at saving lives and improving health on a daily basis. Over 50,000 people around the globe are treated each year with adult stem cells. The diseases and conditions successfully treated by adult stem cells, as shown by published scientific evidence, continue to expand, with published success for numerous cancers, spinal cord injury, heart damage, multiple sclerosis, sickle cell anemia, and many others.

Here are a few samples of adult stem cell advances in the last year.

French scientists showed for the first time that a few adult stem cells from a patient could be used to grow enough red blood cells in the lab for a transfusion.

Heart damage. Adult stem cells continue to pile up the evidence for their success at improving the health of damaged hearts. Repair of damaged heart muscle in patients has been documented both for new heart attack damage as well as for patients with chronic heart failure. Doctors at Cedars-Sinai Hospital in Los Angeles used adult stem cells from the hearts of the patients themselves, grown in the lab and then injected back into the patients' own hearts. They found that the adult stem cells could regrow damaged heart muscle and reduce scars in the heart tissue. Meanwhile Yale [University] scientists used a young girl's own bone marrow adult stem cells to grow heart tissue and blood vessels to repair the girl's congenital heart problem. And doctors from the Texas Heart Institute in Houston presented evidence that adult stem cells from a patient's own bone marrow could repair damaged areas of hearts suffering from severe heart failure, allowing the heart to increase its pumping capacity to deliver oxygenated blood to the body. If you think that using adult stem cells to treat heart damage is a new fad or unproven in the medical literature, you need to understand that it's not. Prof. Dr. med. Bodo-Eckehard Strauer of Germany recently published a review of his own and other's clinical trials, starting with his first adult stem cell transplant for a heart patient back in 2001.

Muscle repair. Scientists at the University of Pittsburgh School of Medicine have shown that adult stem cells from the muscle of young mice can improve the health and extend the life of aged mice. While this doesn't mean that the cells are truly the fountain of youth, it highlights the possibility of using adult stem cells for muscle repair, as well as the ability eventually to isolate "rejuvenating factors" from adult stem cells in muscle or other tissues.

New windpipes. Italian Dr. Paolo Macchiarini, who is a Visiting Professor at the Karolinska Institute in Stockholm, Sweden, continues to improve on his procedure to grow new windpipes for patients. Dr. Macchiarini has grown new trachea for at least eight patients, using the patient's own adult stem cells from bone marrow to grow functional windpipes in patients with cancer or other tracheal problems. His most recent advance this year was using a synthetic substrate on which the adult stem cells are seeded, allowing them to grow and take the shape of a normal windpipe.

Grow your own transfusion. French scientists showed for the first time that a few adult stem cells from a patient could be used to grow enough red blood cells in the lab for a transfusion. The adult stem cells efficiently produced new cells that survived transfusion back into the patient's body and functioned normally.

4

Reprogrammed Adult Cells Are Not an Alternative to Embryonic Stem Cells

Lara Salahi

Lara Salahi covers breaking medical news and health and wellness for ABCNews.com, Good Morning America, *and* World News with Diane Sawyer.

Recently some scientists have proposed that reprogrammed adult stem cells, known as induced pluripotent stem (iPS) cells, can be made to function in a way that is similar to embryonic stem cells. This would allow cells from one type of tissue to be refashioned into cells of other tissue types. However, research to prove this has not been successful. Two recently released studies suggest that adult and embryonic stem cells should not be considered interchangeable.

Adult tissues that are reprogrammed to become stem cells may not be the blank slate that researchers find in other stem cell types, further questioning whether adult cells can be considered a reliable alternative for embryonic stem cells, according to two new studies published Monday [July 19, 2010] in *Nature* and *Nature Biotechnology.*

In one study, researchers at Children's Hospital in Boston, genetically engineered adult tissues in mice to imitate embryonic stem cells. They found these reprogrammed cells, known

Edited from: Lara Salahi, "Reprogrammed Adult Cells Are Not an Alternative to Embryonic Stem Cells," ABC News, July 20, 2010. Copyright © 2010 by ABC News. All rights reserved. Reproduced by permission. This piece was edited. No promotional use allowed.

as induced pluripotent stem (IPS) cells, meant to act as blank cells, actually retained characteristics of the tissue that it once was.

"We're finding that there's a subtle memory of where the [adult] cells came from," said Dr. George Daley, director of the stem cell transplantation program at Children's Hospital and lead researcher of one of the studies.

Induced pluripotent stem cells made from reprogrammed adult cells may not be equivalent to embryonic stem cells, as many researchers once thought.

Reprogrammed Adult Cells Are Not a Blank Slate

Stem cells are heralded as a tabula rasa [blank slate] that can be fashioned into healthy organs and other tissues to potentially treat diseases. Adult cells are often used to reproduce cells of its origin, while embryonic stem cells are not limited to a specific tissue type.

However, both studies suggest that induced pluripotent stem cells made from reprogrammed adult cells may not be equivalent to embryonic stem cells, as many researchers once thought.

"We thought we could reset [blood cells] so we can make a bone tissue or other tissue types, and realized it [did] not make a bone tissue as well. But it did well going back to a blood cell," said Daley.

Researchers currently use adult stem cells to treat genetic diseases. For example, adult blood cells are used to treat genetic blood diseases such as leukemia, and skin cells may be used to regenerate skin tissue and heal otherwise fatal wounds.

"It's an advantage when you want to make the same tissue type, but not if you're looking at making something new," said Daley.

While induced pluripotent stem cells are not yet used in practice, researchers are exploring ways that any adult cell can be reprogrammed into stem cells and refashioned into any type of tissue in the body, regardless of where it was originally taken.

According to Ihor Lemischka, director of the Black Family Stem Cell Institute at Mount Sinai School of Medicine, these studies suggest that induced pluripotent stem cells may more likely resemble adult tissue cells rather than embryonic stem cells.

"If you make an IPS cell from skin cells and you want to use that for studying blood diseases, then we know now that you might be better off starting with blood tissue instead," said Lemischka.

Furthering the Argument for Continued Stem Cell Research

While the ethical debate rages over whether reprogrammed stem cells may effectively substitute for embryonic stem cells, many experts said the studies released Monday confirm that each cell type, adult or embryonic, should not be considered interchangeable.

"The take home message is that what stem cell biologists have been arguing for years is true—that we need to continue studying both stem cells, because we don't know which cells can be used for which applications," said Sean Morrison, director of the Center for Stem Cell Biology at the University of Michigan.

Although Daley's research suggested that cells refashioned into pluripotent stem cells still remember its original tissue structure, Morrison said these cells could still be useful for other types of therapies besides ones that need embryonic stem cells or adult tissue cells.

"In the end, adult stem cells will probably prove superior for certain therapeutic applications, reprogrammed cells might work for other applications, and embryonic cells for others," said Morrison.

While some studies suggest that each stem cell type contains unique features that are not identical to another type, Morrison said many similarities and differences of each stem cell type are not well understood.

"These are some of the first studies to suggest that there really are important differences," said Morrison.

Lemischka said understanding the comparative features of each type of stem cell will help researchers find the potential benefits of all.

"The main impact of IPS technology will be to develop reliable and robust ways to model and study disease," said Lemischka. "And that will lead to making suitable cell populations to study drugs that hopefully will [treat diseases]."

But to do that, Daley said it is important to continue researching embryonic stem cells to find how to better manipulate induced pluripotent stem cells.

"It's at great risk to the progress of the field, to ignore the lessons that embryonic stem cells still have to teach us," said Daley.

5

Reprogrammed Adult Stem Cells Raise New Ethical Issues

Matthew Hoberg

Matthew Hoberg is pursuing a doctoral degree in philosophy at the University of California, Berkeley.

Induced pluripotent stem (iPS) cells are believed by some to offer a way around the ethical issues associated with embryonic stem cells, which require the destruction of human embryos. However, iPS technology brings its own ethical complications. The new method of creating induced pluripotent stem cells allows for "gameteless reproduction," or reproduction without the use of reproductive cells from humans, thus severing the intrinsic connection between conception and familial relationship. It also raises questions about the reproductive choices of the disabled. With the very real possibility of new advances in human reproduction as a result of iPS cells, we must establish a sound body of law governing stem cell research and tissue donation.

Scientists have recently developed a safe and efficient method to create induced pluripotent stem (iPS) cells from adult skin cells. Many opponents of embryonic stem cell research hail this news as an important step away from research methods that rely on destroying embryos. Despite this advance, the future of iPS cell research involves challenging moral and legal issues.

Matthew Hoberg, "The Moral Frontiers of Stem Cell Research," The Public Discourse: Ethics, Law and the Common Good, December 6, 2010. www.thepublicdiscourse.com. Copyright © 2010 by The Witherspoon Institute. All rights reserved. Reproduced by permission.

The therapeutic promise of stem cell research rests on using pluripotent stem cells, which can be grown into many of the types of cells found in the human body. Until recently, such cells could be produced only by destroying human embryos and harvesting embryonic stem cells. Opponents of embryonic stem cell research (ESCR) sought a method of producing pluripotent cells without destroying embryos. Their goal was to show that adult cells, rather than embryos, could provide the raw material for stem-cell therapy.

The Future Is Now

In 2007, scientists demonstrated that they could transform human skin cells into iPS cells, bypassing the destruction of embryos. While opponents of ESCR hailed this announcement as a sign that iPS cells could provide the full therapeutic promise of ES cells, the methods were still in their infancy. It took about a month for the iPS cells to develop, and very few transformations were successful: 99.9% of treated cells failed to transform. Besides being slow and unreliable, the techniques were dangerous. Viruses were used to insert specific genes into the adult cells, which increased the cancer risk for the stem cells and thus for prospective patients receiving stem cell therapy. Without a safer technique, the promise of iPS cell research remained in the future.

In the long run, fewer embryos may be destroyed in stem-cell research as research shifts to iPS cells; but this transition may take years.

That future is now. On September 30 [2010], researchers led by Derrick J. Rossi, Ph.D., at the Harvard Stem Cell Institute reported a novel technique for producing iPS cells from adult skin cells that is fast, reliable, and safe. Instead of viruses, Rossi's team transformed skin cells using messenger RNA (mRNA), producing iPS cells two times faster and one hundred times more reliably than the virus techniques. Most importantly, the mRNA method does not raise the cancer risk for the iPS cells. While there is still room for improvement in the method's efficiency, scientists in the field view Rossi's discovery as a major breakthrough. Robert Lanza, chief scientific officer at Advanced Cell Technology, likens it to "turning lead into gold."

Opponents of ESCR have applauded the discovery as well, citing its potential to render obsolete research methods that destroy embryos. Richard Doerflinger, Deputy Director of the Secretariat for Pro-Life Activities at the United States Conference of Catholic Bishops, commented: "With each new study it becomes more and more implausible to claim that scientists must rely on destruction of human embryos to achieve rapid progress in regenerative medicine."

With the new mRNA method for producing iPS cells the prospects for iPS cell research are better than ever. In this respect, opponents of ESCR should welcome the news. They should be aware, however, that it is no moral panacea.

Demand Will Continue

To begin with, demand for embryonic stem cells will continue in the near future. In order to determine that the transformations work properly and the cells are safe for therapeutic use, researchers need to compare the iPS cells to ES cells, which means destroying embryos. In the long run, fewer embryos may be destroyed in stem-cell research as research shifts to iPS cells; but this transition may take years.

The moral complications of the new state of the art go even deeper, due to an advance that scientists anticipate within a decade: using iPS cells to create human sperm and egg cells. Scientists will be able to create an entire embryo using ordinary skin cells or other adult cells, without *ever* using gametes harvested from a person. This method, which we might call *gameteless reproduction*, makes in vitro fertilization [IVF] look like child's play and gives us more control than ever over human reproduction. The prospect of gameteless reproduction not only makes even more pressing the ongoing debate about the morality and legality of human cloning, but also raises moral and legal questions that are not widely known and discussed, even among the staunchest opponents of ESCR.

First, there are the moral issues connected with the procedure itself. Like Somatic Cell Nuclear Transfer (SCNT), the method used to clone Dolly [the sheep] in 1996, gameteless reproduction raises the question of the morality of cloning and other kinds of asexual reproduction, since it allows the creation of an embryo from one or more tissue donors. However, gameteless reproduction has the potential to transform reproduction even more dramatically than SCNT. Unlike SCNT, gameteless reproduction uses easily obtainable adult tissue and does not require donated ova, which can be obtained only through a highly invasive procedure. It will thus be a dramatically cheaper and easier route to asexual reproduction, and may therefore be much more widely used than SCNT. Due to its advantage over SCNT, gameteless reproduction may over time replace IVF as the assisted reproductive technology of choice. Since it allows reproduction without donated sperm or eggs, gameteless reproduction expands the possibilities of reproduction. In principle, young children or deceased persons could become parents of embryos used in research. Moreover, gameteless reproduction may erode the link between procreation and any kind of family context: single persons, for example, could create an embryo using only their genetic material. As a result, children could be increasingly—and tragically—viewed as products, rather than the fruit of a loving relationship. Most importantly, like other non-conjugal methods of conception that sever the procreative and unitive aspects of human sexuality, gameteless reproduction is intrinsically immoral.

Despite the anticipated development of gameteless reproduction and the serious moral questions it raises, this technique (like SCNT) is permitted under federal law. Only six states (Arkansas, Indiana, Iowa, Michigan, North Dakota, and South Dakota) have laws against therapeutic cloning, but only the Indiana law is broad enough to cover gameteless reproduction. We should expand existing prohibitions on cloning to cover gameteless reproduction as well.

Prohibiting parents from knowingly conceiving a severely disabled child, on the grounds that their doing so would lead the child to have a life not worth living, expresses profound disrespect for the value of each human life.

Apart from these issues with the procedure itself, gameteless reproduction will also give parents an extraordinary level of control over the genetic makeup of their children. What moral principles govern these choices? Are parents morally required to create the "best" possible children? And should the law prevent parents from choosing to create children with disabilities?

Protecting Human Life

Every human life is worth living, even a life beset by extraordinary hardship or disability. This is the foundation for protecting all human life, including the very young, the very old, and the physically and mentally disabled. It is therefore never wrong, in and of itself, to choose to bring a new human life into existence, though it may be wrong to do so with certain intentions, in certain circumstances, and through certain means. As I said earlier, non-conjugal reproduction is intrinsically immoral, and this is so because it involves an impermissible means of conception. In itself, however, choosing to conceive a child is a fundamentally good act. I therefore reject the view held by Joseph Spoerl (Professor of Philosophy at St.

Anselm College), who has argued that choosing to conceive a child is to treat the future child as a means to the parents' ends, since the child does not yet exist and therefore cannot be benefitted by the choice. On the contrary, in choosing to conceive, parents are taking the necessary first steps for their child to come into existence; provided they are not making these choices for selfish reasons, they are not treating their child as a means only and are acting permissibly. This is a delicate issue, and I firmly agree ... that we need to devote more attention to the intrinsic moral status of reproduction.

In recognition of the goodness of conception in itself, we should protect the choices of parents to have children who share their disabilities. If deaf parents foresee that conceiving a child through a conjugal act would result in a congenitally deaf child, that choice is morally permissible and should be legally protected. It does *not* follow that deliberately choosing a deaf child through embryonic selection is permissible.

Protecting the Disabled

There's another argument in favor of protecting the reproductive choices of the disabled. The law not only governs our behavior but also expresses our values. Prohibiting parents from knowingly conceiving a severely disabled child, on the grounds that their doing so would lead the child to have a life not worth living, expresses profound disrespect for the value of each human life. Importantly, even if it's controversial that every life is worth living, it's arguable that the law should proceed as though it were true because not doing so would dishonor those who live with disabilities. How can society claim to value the deaf, or those with other disabilities, if it requires that their children not resemble them in these respects?

Though it is seldom discussed among opponents of ESCR, there is a further set of issues that gameteless reproduction raises: how should we regulate tissue donation in light of future advances in reproductive technology? Donating tissue for scientific research will soon mean donating tissue that can be used to grow a sperm or egg; tissue donors could then become parents at the whim of the researchers possessing their tissue. While it has always been important for tissue donors to have some control over what procedures are done with their samples—some donors might be comfortable with certain kinds of research, and others might not—informed consent will be more important than ever once a simple cheek swab provides the raw material for someone to be a mother or father. There is disagreement in the courts and legal academy about whether there is a constitutional right not to be a parent; there should be no dispute that it is gravely immoral to make someone a parent (even of the most nascent form of human life, the embryo) without their informed consent.

No Requirement for Informed Consent

The current law governing informed consent for tissue donation is woefully inadequate for protecting tissue donors in light of anticipated progress with iPS cell research. Informed consent is required when donating tissue for therapeutic research, in which the patient stands to benefit from the treatment being tested; violating the informed consent requirement is a tort [wrongful act]. However, when donors give tissue to non-therapeutic research, in which they will not benefit from experimental treatment, violating informed consent is punished through administrative measures, like denial of federal funding. This minor response is clearly inadequate for the moral gravity of using someone's tissue to make them a parent without their consent.

Moreover, once the tissue has been donated, there is no further risk of harm to the donor. This means that there is no legal informed consent requirement whenever obtaining a consent waiver is impractical and the tissue can no longer be linked back to the donor. If these two conditions are met, which is not uncommon, there are no restrictions related to informed consent for how researchers can use a donor's tissue. In the absence of a sufficiently wide ban on human cloning and gameteless reproduction, or a legally protected right not to be a parent, researchers in these scenarios have a legal green light to make tissue donors parents without any kind of consent; this is profoundly immoral and should be a legally actionable tort.

As new advances alter the possibilities of human reproduction, we must develop a morally sound body of law governing stem cell research and tissue donation. Science studies momentum and other physical quantities but it also has its own momentum, which we must harness to promote the common good.

6

Most Americans Support Funding for Embryonic Stem Cell Research

Barack Obama

Barack Obama is the forty-fourth President of the United States.

Embryonic stem cell research offers a promising path of scientific discovery that can potentially lead to life-saving treatments. A consensus has emerged that society should support scientists who are engaged in stem cell research, including research involving embryonic stem cells. US government policy will favor sound science, arrived at in an environment of free and open inquiry.

Today [March 9, 2009], with the Executive Order I am about to sign, we will bring the change that so many scientists and researchers; doctors and innovators; patients and loved ones have hoped for, and fought for, these past eight years: we will lift the ban on federal funding for promising embryonic stem cell research. We will vigorously support scientists who pursue this research. And we will aim for America to lead the world in the discoveries it one day may yield.

At this moment, the full promise of stem cell research remains unknown, and it should not be overstated. But scientists believe these tiny cells may have the potential to help us understand, and possibly cure, some of our most devastating diseases and conditions. To regenerate a severed spinal cord

Barack Obama, "Remarks of President Barack Obama—As Prepared for Delivery; Signing of Stem Cell Executive Order and Scientific Integrity Presidential Memorandum," The White House—Presidential Memorandum, March 9, 2009.

and lift someone from a wheelchair. To spur insulin production and spare a child from a lifetime of needles. To treat Parkinson's, cancer, heart disease and others that affect millions of Americans and the people who love them.

Promising Avenues Must Be Explored

But that potential will not reveal itself on its own. Medical miracles do not happen simply by accident. They result from painstaking and costly research—from years of lonely trial and error, much of which never bears fruit—and from a government willing to support that work. From life-saving vaccines, to pioneering cancer treatments, to the sequencing of the human genome—that is the story of scientific progress in America. When government fails to make these investments, opportunities are missed. Promising avenues go unexplored. Some of our best scientists leave for other countries that will sponsor their work. And those countries may surge ahead of ours in the advances that transform our lives.

The majority of Americans—from across the political spectrum, and of all backgrounds and beliefs—have come to a consensus that we should pursue this research.

But in recent years, when it comes to stem cell research, rather than furthering discovery, our government has forced what I believe is a false choice between sound science and moral values. In this case, I believe the two are not inconsistent. As a person of faith, I believe we are called to care for each other and work to ease human suffering. I believe we have been given the capacity and will to pursue this research—and the humanity and conscience to do so responsibly.

It is a difficult and delicate balance. Many thoughtful and decent people are conflicted about, or strongly oppose, this research. I understand their concerns, and we must respect their point of view.

But after much discussion, debate and reflection, the proper course has become clear. The majority of Americans— from across the political spectrum, and of all backgrounds and beliefs—have come to a consensus that we should pursue this research. That the potential it offers is great, and with proper guidelines and strict oversight, the perils can be avoided.

That is a conclusion with which I agree. That is why I am signing this Executive Order, and why I hope Congress will act on a bi-partisan basis to provide further support for this research. We are joined today by many leaders who have reached across the aisle to champion this cause, and I commend them for that work.

Ultimately, I cannot guarantee that we will find the treatments and cures we seek. No President can promise that. But I can promise that we will seek them—actively, responsibly, and with the urgency required to make up for lost ground. Not just by opening up this new frontier of research today, but by supporting promising research of all kinds, including groundbreaking work to convert ordinary human cells into ones that resemble embryonic stem cells.

By doing this, we will ensure America's continued global leadership in scientific discoveries.... That is essential not only for our economic prosperity, but for the progress of all humanity.

I can also promise that we will never undertake this research lightly. We will support it only when it is both scientifically worthy and responsibly conducted. We will develop strict guidelines, which we will rigorously enforce, because we cannot ever tolerate misuse or abuse. And we will ensure that our government never opens the door to the use of cloning for human reproduction. It is dangerous, profoundly wrong, and has no place in our society, or any society.

Free and Open Inquiry Must Be Protected

This Order is an important step in advancing the cause of science in America. But let's be clear: promoting science isn't just about providing resources—it is also about protecting free and open inquiry. It is about letting scientists like those here today do their jobs, free from manipulation or coercion, and listening to what they tell us, even when it's inconvenient— especially when it's inconvenient. It is about ensuring that scientific data is never distorted or concealed to serve a political agenda—and that we make scientific decisions based on facts, not ideology.

By doing this, we will ensure America's continued global leadership in scientific discoveries and technological break-throughs. That is essential not only for our economic prosperity, but for the progress of all humanity.

That is why today, I am also signing a Presidential Memorandum directing the head of the White House Office of Science and Technology Policy to develop a strategy for restoring scientific integrity to government decision making. To ensure that in this new Administration, we base our public policies on the soundest science; that we appoint scientific advisors based on their credentials and experience, not their politics or ideology; and that we are open and honest with the American people about the science behind our decisions. That is how we will harness the power of science to achieve our goals—to preserve our environment and protect our national security; to create the jobs of the future, and live longer, healthier lives.

As we restore our commitment to science, and resume funding for promising stem cell research, we owe a debt of gratitude to so many tireless advocates, some of whom are with us today, many of whom are not. Today, we honor all those whose names we don't know, who organized, and raised awareness, and kept on fighting—even when it was too late for them, or for the people they love. And we honor those we know, who used their influence to help others and bring attention to this cause—people like Christopher and Dana Reeve [actor Christopher Reeve and his wife Dana actively lobbied in support of embryonic stem cell research], who we wish could be here to see this moment.

One of Christopher's friends recalled that he hung a sign on the wall of the exercise room where he did his grueling regimen of physical therapy. It read: "For everyone who thought I couldn't do it. For everyone who thought I shouldn't do it. For everyone who said, 'It's impossible.' See you at the finish line."

Christopher once told a reporter who was interviewing him: "If you came back here in ten years, I expect that I'd walk to the door to greet you."

Christopher did not get that chance. But if we pursue this research, maybe one day—maybe not in our lifetime, or even in our children's lifetime—but maybe one day, others like him might.

There is no finish line in the work of science. The race is always with us—the urgent work of giving substance to hope and answering those many bedside prayers, of seeking a day when words like "terminal" and "incurable" are finally retired from our vocabulary.

Today, using every resource at our disposal, with renewed determination to lead the world in the discoveries of this new century, we rededicate ourselves to this work.

Thank you, God bless you, and may God bless America.

7

The Catholic Church Supports Adult Stem Cell Research

John Monczunski

John Monczunski is an associate editor of Notre Dame Magazine.

The Catholic Church opposes embryonic stem cell research. The University of Notre Dame has, however, undertaken many scientific research projects that involve the use of other kinds of stem cells, such as adult and iPS (induced pluripotent stem) cells. Groundbreaking projects involving these stem cells are aimed at combating blindness, arthritis, blood disorders, and other diseases.

Notre Dame [ND] scientists and engineers are engaged in a number of groundbreaking biomedical research projects aimed at combating blindness, arthritis, blood disorders and a host of other diseases. The common denominator in all this work is an unusual class of cells that might be thought of as Mother Nature's duct tape, the thing that can become anything and fix anything.

Stem cells are undifferentiated cells that serve the body as the universal building block and repair kit. In effect, they can become any of the specialized cells of the body's various tissues and organs. With so much potential, the hope has been that one day they may unlock the secrets of human development and yield powerful therapies to treat a wide variety of

John Monczunski, "Exploring the Medical Promise of Stem Cells," *Notre Dame Magazine*, Winter 2009. Copyright © 2009 by Notre Dame Magazine. All rights reserved. Reproduced by permission.

genetic disorders and diseases, including cancer, heart disease, Alzheimer's, Parkinson's and more.

Yet for as much promise as they hold, they have been shrouded in controversy. The Catholic Church and others have had moral misgivings about certain types of stem cells. In this context, it is important to note that absolutely none of the research conducted at [the University of] Notre Dame violates Church teaching on the sanctity of life.

Only research using embryonic stem cells has been condemned by the Church. The Church is opposed to their use because human embryos must be destroyed to acquire them.

When it comes to the ethics of stem cells, not all are created equally. "The crucial issue is their source," says Phil Sloan, the Notre Dame professor of liberal studies whose field is the philosophy and history of science.

Stem cells come in three varieties: embryonic, adult and what are called induced pluripotent or iPS cells. Of the three types, Sloan points out that only research using embryonic stem cells has been condemned by the Church. The Church is opposed to their use because human embryos must be destroyed to acquire them. The other types of stem cells are derived from adult tissue and therefore not morally problematic.

Catholic Church Approval

"Contrary to what some may believe, the Church is not opposed to all forms of stem cell research or the therapeutic use of stem cells," the philosopher notes. In fact, the Vatican [governing body of the Catholic Church in Rome, Italy] has actively encouraged adult stem cell research. Echoing Rome, in their statement "On Embryonic Stem Cell Research," the U.S.

Conference of Catholic Bishops cited the use of adult stem cells as a "better way" to achieve the therapeutic promise of stem cells.

"There is no moral objection to research and therapy of this kind when it involves no harm to human beings at any stage of development and is conducted with appropriate informed consent," the bishops wrote.

Against this backdrop, Notre Dame is actively engaged in exploring this "better way."

Actually, some of the most advanced and promising stem cell research taking place at Notre Dame doesn't even involve human cells. Stem cells from fruit flies, tropical fish and mice have been yielding answers to important medical questions in ND labs for some time.

For instance, adult neuronal stem cells from the zebrafish, an inch-long tropical fish with five blue stripes on the side of its body, have helped Professor David Hyde and his colleagues to gain a better understanding of the development and regeneration of the retina. A full understanding of the mechanism might one day make it possible to repair human retinal damage, such as that caused by macular degeneration, glaucoma and other retinal diseases that lead to blindness.

Additionally, Hyde points out that since these same neuronal stem cells exist in the brain, a full understanding of the regeneration mechanism might one day also lead to therapies for diseases that destroy brain tissue, such as Parkinson's.

Professor Robert Schulz, meanwhile, has been studying fruit fly stem cells to gain a better understanding of the biochemical processes involved in blood cell production. Specifically, Schulz is screening the fruit fly's genetic makeup to discover which genes are involved in triggering stem cells to become blood cells. A knowledge of these genes will reveal the biochemical mechanisms involved, which in turn is crucial to understanding blood diseases and cancers such as leukemia.

On another front, mechanical engineering professors Diane Wagner, Glen Niebur and Ryan Roeder are engaged in a variety of research projects working with mesenchymal cells from mice. These are a type of adult stem cell that differentiates into the specialized cells of bone, cartilage and fat. Their work has implications for treating arthritis and various orthopedic disabilities.

Through the Mammalian Induced Pluripotent Stem Cell Consortium at ND, Professor Malcolm Fraser is helping to advance work with iPS cells, which are adult differentiated cells, such as skin cells, that are reverse engineered to have the advantages of embryonic stem cells without the moral concerns.

Several years ago Fraser and his colleagues discovered a certain genetic element that other scientists have used to circumvent a serious drawback with the conventional method of creating iPS cells. Namely, PiggyBac, as the snippet of DNA is known, inserts then removes a cancer-causing gene used in the process. In the conventional method, the cancer gene remains in the cell.

A workshop is being planned ... to examine the ethical dimensions of stem cell research and develop a rationale for preferring adult stem cell research over what some have termed "destructive" embryonic research.

Ethical View

Notre Dame's interest in stem cell technology, however, is not confined to the science of the cells. The University recently launched an interdisciplinary adult stem cell initiative, offering seed grants to encourage ND faculty to expand their work in the area. The effort aims at fostering scholarship and training along the legal and ethical dimensions of stem cell research as well as science.

"We are on the frontier of some pretty important work that can relieve a lot of human suffering, so it's essential to engage the moral and legal issues as well as the science," says Robert Bernhard, Notre Dame vice president for research.

In addition to scientific stem cell research, the University hopes to offer training to humanities, law and science graduate students.

"By coalescing our faculty in this area we hope to educate our science and engineering graduate students with a moral and ethical background in this work. At the same time, we hope to offer those in arts and letters and the law a scientific foundation from which to base their own work," says Hyde, who directs the Center for Zebrafish Research.

For instance, a workshop is being planned for summer 2011 to bring together scientists and other scholars to examine the ethical dimensions of stem cell research and develop a rationale for preferring adult stem cell research over what some have termed "destructive" embryonic research.

"It will be an opportunity to think about some deeper philosophical issues related to this, with the intent of making a more compelling case to the biomedical research community," Sloan says.

•

8

The Stem Cell War

David Klinghoffer

David Klinghoffer is a senior fellow at the Discovery Institute.

Despite extravagant claims about the promise of embryonic stem cell research, no effective therapies have yet been developed. Adult stem cell research, on the other hand, has resulted in many significant advances that have not been fully reported by the media. The real war is not a "war on science," but a war on truth.

An enduring liberal myth, that of the Republican "war on science," got a subtle rebuke this week when the first and only patient to receive FDA-approved embryonic-stem-cell therapy publicly revealed his identity. Timothy J. Atchison, a 21-year-old nursing student, had been partially paralyzed in a car crash. Six months ago, scientists at the Shepherd Center in Atlanta sought to test on him the safety of a drug concocted from stem cells of the kind derived by destroying a human embryo.

Are you surprised to learn that this was the very first such clinical test of embryonic-stem-cell research (ESCR)? The news story about Timothy Atchison reminds us that unlike therapies from morally unobjectionable adult stem cells, embryonic stem cells so far have not cured anyone of anything.

"The Republican war on science" is a catchy phrase coined by journalist Chris Mooney in a 2005 book of the same name. According to the pervasively influential mythology, religious

David Klinghoffer, "The Stem-Cell War," *National Review*, April 13, 2011. Copyright © 2011 by the National Review. All rights reserved. Reproduced by permission.

and other conservatives stand athwart medicine—and good science in other fields, too—in a campaign to force their antiquated beliefs on other people.

Well, let's see now. Successful medical research has tangible results. People are healed, or they are not. From the hype that ESCR has received since 2001, when President Bush limited federal funding for it—a move reversed by President Obama— you might think it has shown the capacity to perform miracles. If so, you've been deceived.

Perhaps deliberately. In Minnesota right now, state GOP lawmakers are trying to ban the cloning of human embryos, a technology tied to embryonic-stem-cell research. Critics of the legislation say it's just another instance of the war on science. To prove it, they brought forward a woman, Trisha Knuth, whose little boy, Charlie, has been relieved of a horrific skin disease by a stem-cell transplant.

The only problem with this story is that the therapy that healed Charlie uses *adult* stem cells, from a donor. Yet when Charlie's mother testified impassionedly to the Minnesota legislature, you had to search carefully in media reports for the information that her son's healing actually had no connection with embryonic stem cells.

Embryonic-stem-cell research, ongoing for 30 years and lavishly funded by the National Institutes of Health, has no record of healing.

"That happens *all* the time!" an exasperated Dr. Theresa Deisher told me. Deisher is the Stanford-trained biotech researcher whose lawsuit last year shut down government funding of ESCR for 17 days. I discovered that the controversial scientist, profiled recently in the journal *Nature* as the "Sarah Palin of stem cells," works just up the street from me in Seattle. "People are treated with adult stem cells and they twist the story to promote embryonic stem cells," she said.

Deisher's lawsuit pointed to legislation passed yearly by Congress, the Dickey-Wicker amendment, that forbids government funding of research that entails the destruction of human embryos. In August, a federal judge issued a preliminary injunction in her favor. The case will probably be resolved by the Supreme Court.

Deisher argues that far from being in conflict with medicine's mission, traditional moral concerns are strongly in line with it. Embryonic-stem-cell research, ongoing for 30 years and lavishly funded by the National Institutes of Health, has no record of healing. Yet morally unproblematic adult stem cells have worked wonders—notably in other countries. U.S. federal funding for trials of novel treatments using these less politically correct stem cells has lagged.

Another researcher, neuroscientist Jean Peduzzi-Nelson of Wayne State University, testified before the U.S. Senate Appropriations Committee in September about the peer-reviewed but underreported advances that have been made using adult stem cells. In Portugal, several years before Timothy Atchison's accident, a young man paralyzed by a severe spinal-cord injury was healed to the point of being able to walk 30 feet unassisted.

In the United States, too, reports the *New England Journal of Medicine*, patients suffering from corneal blindness can now see, and others suffering from sickle-cell anemia have gone years without symptoms. In 2003, at Northwestern Memorial Hospital in Chicago, a man with multiple sclerosis received adult stem cells, and his symptoms disappeared in four months.

We can do well, helping people to *get* well, by doing good and refraining from doing harm to innocent life. How unfortunate that when it comes to treatments with *adult* stem cells—for stroke, diabetes, epilepsy, Parkinson's disease, and other maladies—the government is reluctant to make an adequate investment.

The dilemma that pits medicine against conservatism or science against religion is as false as the one that, in the climate debate, seeks to put capitalism and the environment in conflict. In a false dilemma, alternatives and gradations are arbitrarily excluded. That's a technique of manipulation popular with activists seeking to drive a wedge between their political opponents and the public.

The real war here is not a war on science. It's a war on truth.

9

The FDA Regulates Stem Cell Products to Protect the Public

US Food and Drug Administration

The US Food and Drug Administration (FDA) is the oldest consumer protection agency in the US federal government. Its central purpose is to protect the public health by assuring the safety of foods, human and veterinary drugs, vaccines and other biological products, and medical devices.

Stem cells, which have the potential to repair, restore, and regenerate damaged cells, may eventually be used to treat and cure many medical disorders and diseases. However, stem cell treatments could also cause further damage. The US Food and Drug Administration regulates stem cells to insure they are safe and effective for their intended use. Patients considering stem cell treatment should inquire as to whether the procedures in question have been reviewed and approved by the FDA.

Stem cell therapies offer the potential to treat diseases or conditions for which few treatments exist.

Stem cells, sometimes called the body's "master cells," are the precursor cells that develop into blood, brain, bones and all of your organs. Their promise in medical treatments is that they have the potential to repair, restore, replace and regenerate cells that could then be used to treat many medical conditions and diseases.

"FDA Warns About Stem Cell Claims," US Food and Drug Administration, FDA.gov, 2012.

But the Food and Drug Administration (FDA) is concerned that the hope that patients have for cures not yet available may leave them vulnerable to unscrupulous providers of stem cell treatments that are illegal and potentially harmful.

FDA cautions consumers to make sure that any stem cell treatment they are considering has been approved by FDA or is being studied under a clinical investigation that has been submitted to and allowed to proceed by FDA.

FDA has approved only one stem cell product, Hemacord, a cord blood-derived product manufactured by the New York Blood Center and used for specified indications in patients with disorders affecting the body's blood-forming system.

Regulation of Stem Cells

FDA regulates stem cells in the U.S. to ensure that they are safe and effective for their intended use.

"Stem cells can come from many different sources and under the right conditions can give rise to many different cell types," says Stephanie Simek, Ph.D., deputy director of FDA's Office of Cellular, Tissue and Gene Therapies.

Stem cells that come from bone marrow or blood are routinely used in transplant procedures to treat patients with cancer and other disorders of the blood and immune system.

Consumers need to be aware that at present—other than cord blood for certain specified indications—there are no [FDA] approved stem cell products.

Umbilical cord blood is collected from a placenta with the birth mother's consent. Cord blood cells are then isolated, processed, and frozen and stored in a cord blood bank for future use. Cord blood is regulated by FDA and cord blood banks must follow regulatory requirements.

But there are many other stem cell products, including other cord blood-derived products, that have been reviewed by FDA for use in investigational studies, says Simek. Investigational products undergo a thorough review process as the sponsor prepares to study the safety and effectiveness of the product in adequate and well-controlled human studies (clinical trials).

As part of this review, the sponsor must show how the product will be manufactured so that FDA can make certain that appropriate steps are being taken to help assure the product's safety, purity and potency. FDA also requires that there be sufficient data generated from animal studies to aid in evaluating any potential risks associated with the use of these products.

Consumers need to be aware that at present—other than cord blood for certain specified indications—there are no approved stem cell products.

Advice for Consumers

- If you are considering stem cell treatment in the U.S., ask your physician if the necessary FDA approval has been obtained or if you will be part of an FDA-regulated clinical study. This also applies if the stem cells are your own. Even if the cells are yours, there are safety risks, including risks introduced when the cells are manipulated after removal.

   "There is a potential safety risk when you put cells in an area where they are not performing the same biological function as they were when in their original location in the body," says Simek. Cells in a different environment may multiply, form tumors, or may leave the site you put them in and migrate somewhere else.

- If you are considering having stem cell treatment in another country, learn all you can about regulations covering the products in that country. Exercise caution before undergoing treatment with a stem cell-based product in a country that—unlike the U.S.—may not require clinical studies designed to demonstrate that the product is safe and effective. FDA does not regulate stem cell treatments used solely in countries other than the United States and typically has little information about foreign establishments or their stem cell products.

10

The FDA Should Not Regulate Stem Cell Products

Robert O. Young

Robert O. Young is a research scientist and the coauthor of several books, including The pH Miracle: Balance Your Diet, Reclaim Your Health *and* The pH Miracle for Diabetes.

The US Food and Drug Administration (FDA) claims that a person's own stem cells, when administered to that person in order to treat, cure, or prevent disease, are drugs and thus fall within its regulatory purview. However, the primary role of adult stem cells is to maintain and repair the tissue in which they are found. Clearly, stem cells are not drugs when they are injected into the person from whom they were drawn. The FDA is exercising power in an area of medical practice where it should not have jurisdiction.

In another outrageous power-grab, FDA [US Food and Drug Administration] says your own stem cells are drugs—and stem cell therapy is interstate commerce because it affects the bottom line of FDA-approved drugs in other states!

We wish this were a joke, but it's the US Food and Drug Administration's latest claim in its battle with a Colorado clinic over its Regenexx-SD™ procedure, a non-surgical treatment for people suffering from moderate to severe joint or bone pain using adult stem cells.

Robert O. Young, "FDA's New Claim: 'Your Body Is a Drug—and We Have the Authority to Regulate It!'" in *Articles of Health* (blog), January 31, 2012. Copyright © 2012 by Robert O. Young. All rights reserved. Reproduced by permission.

FDA's Argument

The FDA asserts in a court document that it has the right to regulate the Centeno-Schultz Clinic for two reasons:

- Stem cells are drugs and therefore fall within their jurisdiction. (The clinic argues that stem cell therapy is the practice of medicine and is therefore *not* within the FDA's jurisdiction!)

- The clinic is engaging in interstate commerce and is therefore subject to FDA regulation because any part of the machine or procedure that originates outside Colorado becomes interstate commerce once it enters the state. Moreover, interstate commerce is substantially affected because individuals traveling to Colorado to have the Regenexx procedure would "depress the market for out-of-state drugs that are approved by FDA."

The implication of the FDA's interpretation of the law, if upheld by the court, would mean that all food, drugs, devices, and biologic or cosmetic products would be subject to FDA jurisdiction.

We discussed the very ambiguous issue of interstate commerce last September [2011]—it's an argument the FDA frequently uses when the basis for their claim is otherwise lacking. As we noted then, the FDA holds that an "interstate commerce" test must be applied to all steps in a product's manufacture, packaging, and distribution. This means that if any ingredient or tool used in the procedure in question was purchased out of state, the FDA would in its view have jurisdiction, just as they would if the final product had traveled across state lines.

This time the FDA just nakedly says in court documents that the agency *wants to protect the market for FDA-approved drugs.* No more beating around the bush—their agenda is right out in the open! This appears to be a novel interpretation of the Food Drug and Cosmetic Act (FD&C), as evidenced by the government's failure to cite any judicial precedent for their argument.

The implication of the FDA's interpretation of the law, if upheld by the court, would mean that all food, drugs, devices, and biologic or cosmetic products would be subject to FDA jurisdiction. The FDA is expanding its reach even to commerce *within the state*, which we argue is far beyond its jurisdiction, in order to protect drug company profits. . . .

The Centeno-Schultz Clinic takes your blood, puts it into a centrifuge machine that separates the stem cells, and a doctor puts them back in your body where there is damaged tissue. The clinic has argued numerous times that stem cells aren't drugs because they are components of the patient's blood from his or her own body.

The FDA says otherwise: "Stem cells, like other medical products that are intended to treat, cure, or prevent disease, generally require FDA approval before they can be marketed. At this time, there are no licensed stem cell treatments." There they go again, saying that components of your body are drugs and they have the authority to regulate them! It's the only way the agency can claim that adult stem cell therapy is within FDA's purview.

However, the agency seems to be of two minds. When *ESPN* magazine was doing a story on stem cell treatments, the FDA stated that US policy is to allow the injection of stem cells that are treated with "minimal manipulation," which federal regulations define as "processing that does not alter the relevant biological characteristics of cells or tissues"—which is certainly the case with the Regenexx clinic.

Despite this policy, FDA has been attacking the clinic for the past four years. They have tried injunctions and demanded inspections in their attempts to make the company bend; this court battle is merely the latest salvo.

Stem Cells and Politics

The primary role of adult stem cells in a living organism is to maintain and repair the tissue in which they are found. The hard part has been to get enough of them. But new technology is giving doctors the ability to obtain more stem cells from a patient than previously thought possible, which is why we're now seeing new treatments. Blood, fat, or tissue is withdrawn from the patient, stem cells are obtained using one of these new processes, and the cells are injected back into the patient where they can repair the patient's tissue.

Behind . . . the latest FDA attempted power grab lies the same problem: a medical system run by special interests under the leadership of the US government.

[Texas] Gov. Rick Perry received this kind of stem cell therapy. We and others noted that the governor's defense of freedom of healthcare choice when it came to his own treatment was starkly at odds with his directive to administer HPV [human papillomavirus] vaccines to young girls against their own (and their parents') wishes. It's also at odds with his support for some of the most egregious witch-hunters on the Texas State Medical Board, which he appoints.

Behind Perry's blatant inconsistency and the latest FDA attempted power grab lies the same problem: a medical system run by special interests under the leadership of the US government, the same government that is supposed to represent "we the people."

11

The Politics of Stem Cell Research Leave Scientists in Doubt

Amy Harmon

Amy Harmon is a Pulitzer Prize-winning journalist. She works as a science and technology correspondent for The New York Times.

Embryonic stem cell research has been subjected to intense ethical scrutiny because the cells can only be obtained through the destruction of a human embryo. President Barack Obama lifted restrictions on the research that were put in place by the George W. Bush administration, but a subsequent lawsuit challenges the legality of using public money for research that involves the destruction of embryos. The political and legal controversy surrounding embryonic stem cell research has complicated the careers of researchers whose work requires the use of embryonic stem cells.

Rushing to work at Cincinnati Children's Hospital Medical Center one recent morning, Jason Spence, 33, grabbed a moment during breakfast to type "stem cells" into Google and click for the last 24 hours of news. It is a routine he has performed daily in the six weeks since a Federal District Court ruling put the future of his research in jeopardy.

Amy Harmon, "Stem Cells in Court, Scientists Fear for Careers," *The New York Times,* October 5, 2010. Copyright © 2010 The New York Times. All rights reserved. Used by permission and protected by the Copyright Laws of the United States. The printing, copying, redistribution, or retransmission of this Content without express written permission is prohibited.

"It's always at the front of my brain when I wake up," said Dr. Spence, who has spent four years training to turn stem cells derived from human embryos into pancreatic tissue in the hope of helping diabetes patients. "You have this career plan to do all of this research, and the thought that they could just shut it off is pretty nerve-racking."

Many of the nation's leading stem cell researchers do not know whether they will receive grants they won years earlier . . . or whether new projects will even be considered.

Thirteen Hundred Jobs Are at Stake

Perhaps more than any other field of science, the study of embryonic stem cells has been subject to ethical objections and shaped by political opinion. But only a year after the [Barack] Obama administration lifted some of the limits imposed by President George W. Bush, a lawsuit challenging the use of public money for the research and a conservative shift in Congress could leave the field more sharply restricted than it has been since its inception a decade ago. At stake are about 1,300 jobs, as well as grants from the National Institutes of Health that this year total more than $200 million and support more than 200 projects.

The turn of events has introduced what researchers say is unprecedented uncertainty to a realm of academic science normally governed by the laws of nature and the rules of peer review.

"We're used to people telling us, 'That was a stupid idea, we're not going to fund it,' and we turn around and think of a better one," said James Wells, who heads the laboratory where Dr. Spence has a postdoctoral position. "But there's nothing we can do about this."

The stem cells, which are thought to have curative potential for many diseases because they can be turned into any kind of tissue in the human body, can be obtained only by destroying a human embryo, which many Americans believe is the equivalent of a life.

A Court Has Blocked Federal Monies

In August [2010], Chief Judge Royce C. Lamberth of Federal District Court for the District of Columbia found that the Obama administration's policy violates a law barring federal financing for "research in which a human embryo or embryos are destroyed, discarded or knowingly subjected to risk of injury or death," and issued an injunction blocking federal money for the research.

Since then, the field's fate has appeared to shift almost weekly as the lawsuit wends its way through the courts. Last week, the government won the right from an appeals court to continue financing the contested research while it appeals the ruling. But there is no telling how the appeals court will ultimately rule, and Judge Lamberth could issue a revised injunction.

Many of the nation's leading stem cell researchers do not know whether they will receive grants they won years earlier through the standard competition, or whether new projects will even be considered. Junior scientists like Dr. Spence, poised to start their own laboratories, are caught in limbo. Senior scientists like Dr. Wells are torn between pursuing research they believe in and protecting students from staking their job prospects on projects they may never be able to complete.

The legal roller coaster is raising stress levels and reducing productivity, researchers say. Instead of tending to their test tubes, they find themselves guessing how each member of the Supreme Court might vote on the case. They are also watching the midterm Congressional elections with new interest—

and with some dismay, since many believe that new legislation will be required for their work to continue.

Under guidelines authorized by both the Bush and Obama administrations, work that leads directly to destroying the embryos cannot be federally financed. The government can, however, support subsequent research on the cell lines created by that process.

For all the hope vested in them, human embryonic stem cells have yet to yield tangible results for patients.

Last year, two scientists filed the lawsuit, arguing that the distinction is a false one and that the guidelines on public financing violated the Dickey-Wicker amendment, first passed in 1996 and renewed by Congress every year since.

No Tangible Results Yet

Moreover, they said, it siphons limited government resources from research on different types of stem cells, which they and other scientists who share a discomfort with embryonic stem cells view as ethically and scientifically superior. For all the hope vested in them, human embryonic stem cells have yet to yield tangible results for patients.

In his ruling, Judge Lamberth agreed that the guidelines violated the 1996 amendment and "threaten the very livelihood" of the plaintiffs.

Embryonic stem cell researchers who stand to lose their federal grants as a result argue that other types of stem cells do not have the same properties, and that all need to be studied regardless to determine which work best. They bristle at the intrusion of judges and politicians into decisions usually addressed by the peer review process, in which experts in a field comment on the merit of an idea and the best get financed.

Yet even some who believe there is a compelling scientific rationale for their research agree that the legal basis for federal financing may be weak. "I was astonished that Congress hadn't dealt with this," said Stephen Duncan, a stem cell researcher at the Medical College of Wisconsin, who stands to lose several million dollars in federal grants depending on the dispensation of the case. "It's like being a little pregnant. You're either breaking the law or you're not."

Mr. Bush, who in 2001 limited federally financed researchers to working on roughly two dozen stem cell lines already in existence, twice vetoed legislation that would have explicitly expressed support for financing the contested research. No such legislation has been introduced under President Obama, but the administration expanded the number of stem cell lines researchers could study.

Some researchers are weighing a switch to the private sector. Others have ordered their students to pay no attention to the news. Others are trying to raise public awareness.

A Missed Opportunity

Advocates of the research now see this as a missed opportunity.

Efforts to rally Congressional support since Judge Lamberth's ruling have failed to gain momentum among Democrats and moderate Republicans heading into the November [2010] elections.

For many, the most recent intrusion of politics into the vaunted scientific meritocracy came as a particular shock because the Obama administration's new guidelines had only months earlier fallen into place.

"The painful thing is that we are being stopped at a time when the velocity of this field of research, thanks to the new administration, was finally going at maximum speed," said Ali H. Brivanlou, a professor at Rockefeller University.

Over the last few weeks, embryonic stem cell scientists have sought alternative financing from private foundations, university administrations and state programs. But the National Institutes of Health, which has a $26 billion budget, is by far the source with the deepest pockets for academic scientists.

Some researchers are weighing a switch to the private sector. Others have ordered their students to pay no attention to the news. Others are trying to raise public awareness.

Yi Sun, 45, of the University of California, Los Angeles, has resorted to frequent meditation.

"I would be in trouble without it," said Dr. Sun, whose stem cell work focuses on an autism disorder called Rett syndrome. Born in China, Dr. Sun said she was now renewing efforts to collaborate with well-financed stem cell biologists there.

12

Physicians Are Treating Patients Using Questionable Stem Cell Therapies

Steve Sternberg

Steve Sternberg is a regular correspondent for USA Today.

Experimental stem cell therapies offer hope for the development of a wide variety of medical treatments in the future, but bone marrow transplantation is the only stem cell therapy that has actually proven successful. Untested and unproven stem cell treatments are widely available, not only in the United States but also in Mexico, China, India, and other countries, for conditions including heart disease, diabetes, stroke, seizures, Parkinson's disease, cerebral palsy, and chronic lung disease. Often, the treatments are costly, and they can be dangerous. Some patients choose not to wait for therapies to be tested if they can find physicians who will treat them now.

Before New York Yankees pitcher Bartolo Colon pulled his hamstring while running from the mound to first base on June 11 [2011] fans would have been forgiven for thinking he had chugged from the Fountain of Youth.

Colon has not completed a full season since 2005 and sat out 2010 to rest his aging and injured right arm. But this season, his fastball is back. His ERA [earned run average], 3.10, was among the tops in the league. On May 30, six days after

Steve Sternberg, "Doctors Offer Unapproved Stem Cell Therapies," *USA Today*, June 29, 2011. Copyright © 2011 Gannett. All rights reserved. Used by permission and protected by the Copyright Laws of the United States. The printing, copying, redistribution, or retransmission of this Content without express written permission is prohibited.

his 39th birthday, he pitched his first shutout in five years, hurling his final pitch at 95 mph.

What lit the fuse on his fastball? An infusion of stem cells, says Joseph Purita, founder of the Institute of Regenerative and Molecular Orthopedics in Boca Raton, Fla., who gave Colon the controversial treatment in the Dominican Republic before baseball season began.

Purita isn't the only doctor offering patients stem cells. Doctors in the U.S. and abroad are now providing untested and unapproved stem cell therapies for ailments ranging from heart disease to emphysema to cerebral palsy. And they swear by them.

Embryonic Stem Cells Hold Special Appeal

"Here's a guy who was fooling around for two years and not getting any better. All of a sudden, you do this procedure and a few weeks later he's dramatically better," Purita says. "There must be something going on here."

Experts liken stem cells to the seeds from which many body tissues grow. If scientists can harness stem cells in healing, researchers say, they can revolutionize medicine. Embryonic stem cells—those derived from human embryos—hold special appeal because they can give rise to every cell type in the human body. More recently, researchers have raised the possibility that "induced" stem cells created from skin cells may have the same potential. As a result, world-class scientists agree that stem cell therapies may someday help to rebuild failing hearts, restore cancer-ravaged tissues, bridge gaps in nerves or regenerate damaged lung tissue.

"We really could repair faulty or damaged tissues," says George Daley, director of stem cell transplantation at Children's Hospital Boston, whose team infuses stem cells into leukemia patients as a component of bone marrow transplants. These transplants, which involve destroying cancerous bone marrow and replacing it with disease-free stem cells, have been the standard of care for leukemia for decades.

Daley says bone marrow transplantation remains the only proven form of stem cell therapy. "Virtually everything else is highly experimental," he says, including the most controversial stem cells of all, those derived from human embryos.

It may seem that Colon's treatment turned back the clock, experts say, but there's no evidence that the infusion had anything to do with it.

"We have no way of knowing even whether stem cells are the active ingredient," Daley says.

Medical history is filled with studies in which sugar pills and sham surgery out-perform the real thing, a phenomenon called the "placebo effect."

Even Purita acknowleges that he can't be sure Colon's improvement resulted from his therapy. "Can I be 100% sure it was the stem cells? No, I can't be sure," says Purita. MLB [Major League Baseball] is investigating to make sure Colon wasn't given any banned substances. Purita says he would never take that risk. He also says he limits his stem cell practice to his orthopedics speciality. "I'm not trying to treat Alzheimer's and strokes."

Yankees spokesman Jason Zillo says Colon declined to comment.

Power of Positive Thinking

Ted Kaptchuk of Harvard Medical School says he's not surprised that some patients appear to benefit from stem cell treatments. That's not necessarily because the treatments work, he says. What matters is that patients *think* they work.

Kaptchuck says medical history is filled with studies in which sugar pills and sham surgery out-perform the real thing, a phenomenon called the "placebo effect." The placebo effect is especially potent in surgery, he says, noting more than 100 studies in which "people do wonderfully on the placebo." In one powerful example, he says, a researcher tracked patients for two years after half had real surgery and half had a sham procedure for arthritis of the knee.

The patients who had fake surgery, Kaptchuck says, "were hopping around, doing great. There was no difference between the sham surgery and the real surgery." He adds: "When you go under the knife, it's like going to a shaman. The only difference is that there are no feathers, there are machines and test tubes."

When patients agree to undergo unapproved therapies, they are taking a leap of faith, based on little more than the word of their doctors and the encouragement of other patients.

An Internet search for "stem cells" will turn up a roster of doctors who offer purported stem cell treatments. Most use adult cells from the patients themselves. No one knows how safe or effective the procedures are, researchers say, because few, if any, of the doctors now offering them to patients have tested them scientifically.

"It's a case where the hype is ahead of the science," says Gary Green of UCLA [University of California, Los Angeles], medical director of Major League Baseball.

Even doctors working on FDA [US Food and Drug Administration]-approved stem cell clinical trials are still figuring out how to formulate treatments, deliver them effectively and achieve maximum potency. Reliable therapy is years away. When patients agree to undergo unapproved therapies, they are taking a leap of faith, based on little more than the word of their doctors and the encouragement of other patients.

"We'd all love easy miracles," says Larry Goldstein, head of stem cell research at the University of California-San Diego. "That's not the way it works."

Cells from the Patient

In most cases, stem cell doctors extract the cells directly from the patient's blood, fatty tissue or bone marrow. They use standard laboratory methods to separate them from the blood or other substances. Doctors at some offshore clinics may also obtain stem cells from umbilical cord blood or, in rare cases, human embryos. Doctors then inject or infuse the slurry of concentrated cells back into the patient, where, both doctor and patient hope they'll promote healing. These approaches—especially the use of human embryonic stem cells—have not been approved by the Food and Drug Administration.

> *FDA guidelines limit its authority to regulate treatments involving cells that are withdrawn from a patient and then infused the same day with only "minimal manipulation."*

The most coveted stem cells are those from embryos, which can morph into any cell in the human body. The [George W.] Bush administration, to discourage embryo destruction, put strict controls on embryonic stem cell use.

The government would only fund research using certain batches of stem cells that had already been harvested from embryos. The [Barack] Obama administration lifted those restrictions, expanding federal funding of embryonic stem cell research. The move was temporarily blocked by a judge, but on April 29 [2011], the U.S. Court of Appeals for the D.C. Circuit overturned the ruling and threw open the doors to more federal funding. Those restrictions only applied to research funded by the government, not studies carried out by privately funded biotech firms. Most studies, public and private, are just getting underway.

FDA regulations have loopholes, Goldstein says. FDA guidelines limit its authority to regulate treatments involving cells that are withdrawn from a patient and then infused the same day with only "minimal manipulation." Last August [2010], in a test of its authority, the FDA requested an injunction from the U.S. District Court in Washington, D.C., to block a Broomfield, Colo., orthopedic clinic, Regenerative Sciences, from formulating treatments of cultured stem cells.

The clinic's medical director, Christopher Centeno, says he has repeatedly sued the FDA, arguing that these treatments fall within FDA guidelines for the practice of medicine. The FDA countered with its own lawsuit. The dispute won't be decided until 2013, Centeno says. The FDA declined to comment because the case is pending.

Centeno says he is trying to move stem cell therapy into the mainstream. He helped establish the International Cellular Medicine Society, which drafted guidelines for stem cell treatments and promotes responsible research, he says.

Many patients say they can't, or won't, wait years for scientists to gather evidence, as long as there are doctors willing to treat them now.

The group does not yet accept members, but about 1,500 people, half of them doctors and half patients, have signed up for information, says David Audley, the group's executive director. Two clinics in the U.S. are going through the group's stem cell accreditation process. The group's goal, Audley says, is to assure patient safety, by tracking patients for up to 20 years through a patient registry. "At this point, we don't have enough data to talk about true efficacy," he says. "We would love to get into efficacy."

Buyer Beware

Buyer beware, warns Daley, who is also the head of the International Society for Stem Cell Research, an academic group that posts a cautionary handbook for consumers on its website.

"On one hand," he says, "there are charlatans selling snake oil. At the other end of the spectrum are physicians who may be well intentioned, but they're misinformed if they're giving patients stem cells before they've been proven to work."

Many patients say they can't, or won't, wait years for scientists to gather evidence, as long as there are doctors willing to treat them now.

Barbara Hanson, founder of the online discussion forum Stem Cell Pioneers, says stem cells have allowed her to rebound from life-threatening pulmonary disease and resume an essentially normal life.

"We're not going to sit here and just die, and wait for the FDA to give its stamp of approval for us to have our stem cells used," she says.

Increasingly, doctors find themselves treating critically ill patients who sought stem cells first.

Clinics are flourishing in the USA, Mexico, China, India, the Dominican Republic, Thailand, Russia and the United Kingdom, says Tim Caulfield, a University of Alberta, Canada, law professor who has studied "direct-to-consumer" Internet marketing of stem cells. Caulfield's team found that most websites play up the benefits and downplay the risks of stem cell therapy.

The average cost of care: just under $50,000. Nearly half of those treated were under 18, he says. Parents often fly children to clinics in other countries for untested stem cell treatments for such ailments as autism and cerebral palsy.

"It makes me angry," he says. "They're trading on the excitement of stem cells to market these therapies all over the world, for everything you can think of," including autism, multiple sclerosis, blindness, heart disease, cancer, neurological disorders, even aging. "I regard that as a marker for quackery. If they treat everything, you know it's too good to be true."

Increasingly, doctors find themselves treating critically ill patients who sought stem cells first.

Cleveland Clinic heart specialist Wael Jaber says he was "astonished" when a 75-year-old patient told him he paid $50,000 for stem cell treatments to heal his ailing heart. Two Mayo Clinic lung experts, Charles Burger and Neal Patel, say a pair of their patients paid roughly the same amount for stem cells to treat a deadly lung disease.

"They paid cash, 50 to 60 grand, in advance," Burger says. Medical tests showed that none of the three benefited from the therapy, Jaber and Burger say.

Jaber says his patient—who had triple bypass surgery June 1 [2011]—sought his stem cells at The Brain Therapeutics Medical Clinic in Mission Viejo, Calif., run by osteopath David Steenblock, who advertises on a website called StemcellMD.org.

Steenblock says he treats patients with heart disease, diabetes, stroke, seizures, Parkinson's disease, cerebral palsy, Lou Gehrig's disease (ALS), kidney failure and chronic lung disease. He refers some patients to a clinic in Mexico.

Steenblock's record is anything but unblemished. California Osteopathic Medical Board records show that the board revoked Steenblock's license in 2009 for gross negligence, excessive prescribing and dishonesty while treating a stroke patient with hyperbaric oxygen, which is also controversial. The revocation was stayed; Steenblock may continue to practice medicine, but he was placed on five years' probation, during which he was required to take a course in medical ethics.

Steenblock acknowleged the judgement against him, but said his license is "unfettered" and he's appealing the ruling.

Steven Nissen, chief of cardiology at the Cleveland Clinic, was so incensed when Jaber told him about his stem cell patient that he fired off a letter of complaint to the FDA. Jaber says he was interviewed by FDA investigators.

Not Approved in the United States

The two Mayo clinic patients told their doctors they had their blood drawn at the Regenocyte Therapeutic clinic in Bonita Springs, Fla., run by Zannos Grekos. Grekos says he sent the blood to Israel for processing. It was then shipped to a hospital in Santo Domingo, the Dominican Republic, where the cells were infused into the patients.

Grekos also has had his problems with state regulators. On Feb. 23 [2011], the Florida Board of Medical Examiners filed an emergency order blocking Grekos from providing stem cell therapy in Florida. The state took action after Grekos infused bone marrow cells into the "cerebral circulation" of a 69-year-old woman suffering from a stroke.

The woman, who got the infusion as an outpatient, fell at home that evening and later died of injuries from her fall, records show. A Florida prosecutor, Robert Milne, charged that the treatment was "entirely experimental" and had no "substantiated medical and/or scientific value."

The challenge . . . is to find a balance between protecting patients and allowing doctors enough latitude to innovate and carry out legitimate research.

"We're going to request a hearing and present our side," Grekos says. He notes that while he can't do stem cell procedures in Florida, he's still doing the infusions in other places, including the Dominican Republic and Athens [Greece].

Steenblock and Grekos reject the criticism of their efforts. "Some (doctors) are more conservative, some are more progressive," Grekos says. "If we didn't have more progressive physicians, medicine wouldn't move forward."

Nevertheless, says Mayo's Burger, "This isn't an approved study or a therapy approved for use in the U.S."

The challenge, he says, is to find a balance between protecting patients and allowing doctors enough latitude to innovate and carry out legitimate research. "You don't want to slam the door on something that in 10 years may have potential for people with end-stage disease," Burger says.

•

13

Texas Regulations for Adult Stem Cell Therapies Will Advance Research

Leeza Rodriguez

Leeza Rodriguez is a staff writer for the website CosmeticSurg-.net.

In April 2012, the Texas Medical Board approved the first set of regulations allowing physicians to offer autologous adult stem cell therapies—therapies using cells from the patient's own body. Some medical researchers view the approval negatively, but many practicing physicians and their patients will benefit from the decision, which permits autologous stem cell therapies to go forward.

While Friday the 13th may be bad luck for some, such was not the case for the U.S. stem cell industry. On Friday, April 13, [2012], the Texas Medical Board (TMB) approved the first set of regulations which will allow physicians to offer autologous adult stem cell therapies. These are stem cells from your own body for your own usage.

The Texas bill was drafted over the past year and the final version was released for public comment in March. After the 30 day public comment period, the bill went for final vote on April 13. The TMB passed the new regulation by a vote of 10 to 4.

Leeza Rodriguez, "Texas Medical Board and WSJ OpEd: Tipping Point for Stem Cell Industry," CosmeticSurg.net, April 18, 2012. www.cosmeticsurg.net/blog/2012/04/18/.
Copyright © 2012 by Cosmeticsurg.net. All rights reserved. Reproduced by permission.

Current FDA Regulations

Although the FDA [US Food and Drug Administration] has published regulations for embryonic stem cells and allogeneic stem cell therapies, there has not been a clear cut FDA pathway for autologous adult stem cell therapies. After years of waiting, some physician practices (ours included) recently received FDA guidance on adipose stem cells, but the rules are not written in stone. Regulations are not official until they become part of the *Federal Register*.

The resulting 'time out' and lack of guidance by the FDA created uncertainty among doctors and forced many patients to seek autologous stem cell therapy abroad. To help bridge the gap, the Texas Medical Board created regulations for autologous adult stem cell therapies, the area not yet formalized by the FDA.

Many practicing physicians view the new regulations as a positive step in innovation and patient treatment.

Unlike embryonic stem cells, adult stem cell therapies have no ethical issues. Adult stem cells can be extracted from bone marrow, adipose fat, umbilical cord blood, dental pulp and other adult tissues. These stem cells have been used to treat a wide range of diseases and injuries. Over 3,000 clinical trials using adult stem cells have taken place over the past few decades.

Texas Stem Cell Regulations

With the new Texas regulations, known as Chapter 198, physicians will be able to perform autologous adult stem cell therapies if they conduct therapies under the supervision of an IRB, or Investigational Review Board. In addition to monitoring patient outcomes, IRB's also have very strict protocols for informed consent which tell the patients that the procedure is experimental and that results are not yet known. In summary, Texas Medical Board 198 regulations include:

- The regulation applies only to stem cell therapies that are not currently regulated by the FDA. Thus, this regulation applies to certain types of autologous adult stem cell therapies. Allogeneic therapies (donor cells) and embryonic stem cell treatments are not applicable as they are already delineated as . . . drugs by the FDA.

- Texas physicians must file an IRB which is affiliated with a hospital or academic institution.

- Texas physicians are NOT required to file an IND (Investigational New Drug Application) with the FDA.

- Informed Consents must be IRB approved and state to the patient that the stem cell therapy is experimental.

- Patient results and follow up care must be reported to the IRB, and doctors must be able to respond to information requests by the Texas Medical Board within 14 days of inquiry.

- A physician can charge a fee for the therapy as long as there are no placebos in the therapy.

Throughout history much medical innovation has come outside of prospective randomized clinical trials.

Reaction to Texas Stem Cell Regulations

While some members of the stem cell research community are unhappy over the Texas Medical Board's decision, many practicing physicians view the new regulations as a positive step in innovation and patient treatment. The difference of opinion between researchers and doctors has to do with each side's tolerance for risks and benefits.

Many scientists assess risks and benefits primarily via pro-spective 'randomized clinical trials' (RCT), a process which is common place for the testing of drugs that will be manufac-tured and distributed to thousands of people. Scientists do not interact with the patient and therefore must control as many variables as possible (randomized clinical trials) in or-der to be assured of the highest possible evidence of safety and efficacy.

But practicing physicians communicate with their patients on a one-to-one basis and are comfortable assessing levels of risk/benefits during their patient's therapy. They do not need every external parameter to be controlled in order to see meaningful levels of safety and efficacy with a therapy. There-fore, throughout history much medical innovation has come outside of prospective randomized clinical trials. Physicians validate findings of safety and efficacy via case reports, non-randomized clinical trials, and a peer review mechanism well established by the medical community. Non randomized clini-cal trials performed outside of the FDA purview can show safety, proof of concept, and enough information about risks and benefits to allow for patients to make informed choices.

The Tug of War Between the FDA and "Practice of Medicine"

Traditionally, the FDA's purview has been the safety of "one-to-many" manufactured products. These are drugs, devices, and donor/allogeneic tissues which are dispensed to many people. On the other hand, autologous stem cell therapy is a 'one-to-one relationship'. This is because the cell or product is only distributed to one person, the patient himself. The risks and benefits of "one-to-one therapy" have traditionally fallen under the purview of 'Practice of Medicine'. Following such precedents, the risks and benefits for autologous therapy should be an issue of consent between you (the patient) and your doctor. And therein lies another reason why the Texas Medical Board has exercised it's authority over autologous stem cell therapy.

The Practice of Medicine is primarily regulated by each state's Medical Board, but doctors are accountable on many levels to many organizations. In addition to the State Medical Board, there are layers of peer review organizations that include professional societies, peer review journals, malpractice insurance carriers, hospital boards, licensing and accreditation agencies, the community, and ultimately a courtroom with a jury.

Equally as important is the fact that the patient interacts with their doctor face to face, and doctors get informed consent from every patient before every procedure. Whether it is a traditional procedure or an experimental procedure, the informed consent is part of the process. During the informed consent process doctors give you an idea about the safety and efficacy of the procedure. If your treatment is experimental, the informed consent outlines that fact.

Wall Street Journal's Op-Ed on the FDA and Stem Cells

But last week there was even more good news for the stem cell sector! A few days after the Texas announcement the *Wall Street Journal* posted an Op-Ed piece written by the former FDA commissioner in support of stem cell therapy.

In the Op-Ed piece the former commissioner, Dr. Andrew von Eschenbach, called for a move toward a 21st-century FDA.

He noted the need to overhaul the current FDA regulations and process for evaluating new technologies such as Regenerative Medicine. Furthermore he called attention to the lawsuit of the FDA against a Colorado physician's right to perform autologous stem cell therapy. In a hat tip to the seriousness of Dr. Centeno's case, the former FDA commissioner pointed out how 'lawyers—*many* lawyers are trying to resolve the dispute'. We have previously written about the issues surrounding U.S. vs. Regenerative Sciences here on this blog. The outcome of this case will no doubt be a landmark decision for the stem cell industry.

Dr. Von Eschenbach further impassioned the stem cell cause when he wrote:

> When I was commissioner of the FDA from 2005 to 2009, I saw firsthand how regenerative medicine offered a cure for kidney and heart failure and other chronic conditions like diabetes. Researchers used stem cells to grow cells and tissues to replace failing organs, eliminating the need for expensive supportive treatments like dialysis and organ transplants. But the beneficiaries were laboratory animals . . . the FDA doesn't have the scientific tools and resources to review complex innovations more expeditiously and pioneer regulatory pathways for state of the art therapies that defy current agency conventions.

In conclusion, this is a tipping point for stem cell therapy. We salute the Texas Medical Board and all the hard work it took to get to this point! It's your own cells and you deserve the right to use them. In Texas, patients now have a choice. You don't have to risk being a placebo in a randomized clinical trial, you can have the therapy, as long as you understand the risks.

14

Texas Stem Cell Rules May Impede Clinical Research

Carrie Arnold

Carrie Arnold is a writer who covers topics in medicine and the sciences.

An April 2012 decision by the Texas Medical Board to regulate the experimental use of adult stem cells is a concern to some scientists. In addition to exposing patients to risks arising from unproven therapies, it is feared that the easier availability of stem cell therapies in physicians' offices will discourage participation in clinical research trials, and thus slow the progress of medical research.

Stem cell researchers in the USA and abroad are reeling from new laws in Texas that commercialise experimental procedures and could attract patients away from clinical trials.

New regulations on the experimental use of adult stem cells recently passed by the Texas Medical Board has returned the ethos of the Wild West to the Lone Star State. Supporters of the rules believe they offer patients seeking stem cell therapies a modicum of protection in a semi-lawless environment, but opponents believe that these regulations actually put patients at greater risk. What is more, critics say, these guidelines could actually hold back progress in stem cell research.

"I think it's outrageous", said Leigh Turner, a bioethicist from the University of Minnesota, MN, USA, who testified at

Carrie Arnold, "Texas Stem Cell Rules May Impede Clinical Research." *The Lancet*, May 2012, vol. 379, no. 9828, p. 1776. Copyright © 2012 by Elsevier. All rights reserved. Reproduced by permission.

the medical board's hearings. "Some of what takes place may not be credible research. It's going to be unproven interventions sold for profit with the veneer of a clinical trial."

The regulations give Texas doctors "a reasonable and responsible degree of latitude in the use of investigational agents", which allows them to offer experimental stem cell procedures without first getting formal approval from the US Food and Drug Administration (FDA). Texas doctors will have to seek approval from an Institutional Review Board (IRB) and obtain informed consent from patients about the experimental nature of the procedure before they can begin.

These regulations actually provide more protection to patients, noted Leigh Hopper, Public Information Officer for the Texas Medical Board. "These treatments are already happening in Texas. The idea was to put in place some sort of framework that would at least involve informed consent for patients and provide some external oversight", Hopper said.

Without adequate controls, scientists have no way of knowing whether the stem cells are effective.

Turner disagrees. He believes that the rules put corporate profits before patient safety. Clinical research trials do not charge patients to participate. Yet in Texas, it is now legal for a company to charge a patient tens of thousands of dollars to undergo a procedure that may or may not be beneficial, Turner said.

Irv Weissman, a stem cell researcher at Stanford University, CA, USA, pointed out that the IRB process required by the new regulations only protects against patient harm; it does not require that physicians show the procedure will be beneficial. FDA regulations, on the other hand, require researchers to indicate how the trial will help patients. "Without FDA oversight, [physicians] don't have to prove efficacy", Weissman said.

The concerns of stem cell researchers and bioethicists go beyond the marketing of false hope. Patients, especially those with terminal diseases, might be especially attracted to potential stem cell clinics in Texas in part because they would not risk being randomised to a placebo group in a clinical trial. With nothing to lose, a promising treatment might be worth the investment. It might not work, true, but they could be reassured of receiving the actual procedure rather than a placebo.

The problem is that double-blind, randomised, placebo-controlled trials are crucial to understanding whether or not a particular procedure is effective, says Douglas Sipp, Science Policy and Ethics Studies Unit Leader at the RIKEN Center for Developmental Biology in Japan. Like any treatment, the administration of stem cells is subject to placebo effects, expectations, and selection bias. Without adequate controls, scientists have no way of knowing whether the stem cells are effective. Stem cell procedures in Texas—Sipp does not call them therapies—are being marketed as treatment without any evidence that they work.

Every patient who receives a commercial stem cell treatment is another patient unable to participate in a clinical trial, both due to lack of interest and their history of previous stem cell treatments. Common illnesses and injuries have a large enough pool of potential participants that clinical trial enrolment probably will not be seriously diminished. But for rarer diseases, like amyotrophic lateral sclerosis and certain orphan diseases, the availability of commercial experimental stem cells could have a much larger impact in trial enrolment, Turner said. Every patient that undergoes a commercialised and unproven stem cell procedure in Texas means that valuable data is lost to scientists trying to identify effective therapies for these diseases.

This could be the new rule's lasting irony: rather than promoting patient health, the regulations could actually impede the development of novel stem cell therapies with a proven track record. "When you introduce alternatives that have a superficial attraction to patients, it kind of undermines the system", Sipp said. "It makes it easier to conduct medical experiments in people that aren't rigorously designed, and makes people pay for the privilege."

Organizations to Contact

The editors have compiled the following list of organizations concerned with the issues debated in this book. The descriptions are derived from materials provided by the organizations. All have publications or information available for interested readers. The list was compiled on the date of publication of the present volume; names, addresses, phone and fax numbers, and e-mail and Internet addresses may change. Be aware that many organizations take several weeks or longer to respond to inquiries, so allow as much time as possible.

American Cancer Society (ACS)
50 Williams St. NW, Atlanta, GA   30303
website: www.cancer.org

The American Cancer Society is a national organization dedicated to eliminating cancer as a major health problem by preventing disease, saving lives, and diminishing suffering. The ACS website provides detailed information on stem cell transplants, including peripheral blood, bone marrow, and cord blood transplants, as a means of treating different forms of cancer.

Genetics and Public Policy Center
1717 Massachusetts Ave. NW, Suite 530
Washington, DC   20036
(202) 663-5971 • fax: (202) 663-5992
website: www.dnapolicy.org

The Genetics and Public Policy Center was created in 2002 at Johns Hopkins University by Pew Charitable Trusts to help policymakers, the press, and the public understand and respond to the challenges and opportunities of genetic medicine and its potential to transform global public health. The center conducts legal research and policy analysis, performs policy-relevant social science research, crafts robust policy options and recommendations, convenes and consults key stakeholders to identify common ground and develop consensus, and influences national genetics programs and policy. Issue Briefs posted on the center's website address stem cell research and policy.

Hastings Center

21 Malcolm Gordon Rd., Garrison, NY   10524-4125
(845) 424-4040 • fax: (845) 424-4545
e-mail: mail@thehastingscenter.org
website: www.thehastingscenter.org

The Hastings Center is an independent, nonpartisan, and nonprofit bioethics research institute founded in 1969. The center's mission is to address fundamental ethical issues in the areas of health, medicine, and the environment. The Hastings Center website includes an extensive collection of articles and other resources exploring the ethics of stem cell research.

Hinxton Group: An International Consortium on Stem Cells, Ethics, and Law

The Johns Hopkins Berman Institute of Bioethics
1809 Ashland Ave., Baltimore, MD   21205
(410) 614-5391
website: www.hinxtongroup.org

The Hinxton Group was formed in 2004 to explore the ethical and policy challenges of transnational scientific collaboration raised by variations in national regulations governing embryo research and stem cell science. The Hinxton Group website is a clearing house for information about international scientific collaboration in the area of stem cell research. Posted information includes an interactive guide to international policies regulating embryonic stem cell research, current news about stem cell law and policy, and links to basic stem cell facts.

International Society for Stem Cell Research (ISSCR)

5215 Old Orchard Rd., Suite 270, Skokie, IL   60077
(224) 592-5700 • fax: (224) 365-0004

e-mail: isscr@isscr.org
website: www.isscr.org

The International Society for Stem Cell Research is a non-profit organization established to promote the exchange of information and ideas relating to stem cells, to encourage research involving stem cells, and to promote professional and public education in all areas of stem cell research and application. The ISSCR website provides an extensive list of scientific resources related to stem cell research, including stem cell basics, stem cell treatments and "The Stem Cell Classroom," as well as information on ethics and public policy.

National Center for Biotechnology Information (NCBI)
National Library of Medicine, Building 38A
Bethesda, MD   20894
website: www.ncbi.nlm.nih.gov

The National Center for Biotechnology Information is a division of the National Library of Medicine (NLM) at the National Institutes of Health (NIH). As a national resource for molecular biology information, NCBI's mission is to develop new information technologies to aid in the understanding of fundamental molecular and genetic processes that control health and disease. Resources on the NCBI website include a "Science Primer" that provides basic information on bioinformatics and molecular genetics.

National Committee for a Human Life Amendment (NCHLA)
1500 Massachusetts Ave. NW, Suite 24
Washington, DC   20005
(202) 393-0703 • fax: (202) 347-1383
e-mail: Info@nchla.org
website: www.nchla.org

The National Committee for a Human Life Amendment is committed to a civil rights struggle to secure the right-to-life for the unborn child. The organization's website includes information about stem cell research and umbilical cord blood banks. NCHLA produces educational and program resources, communicates with leaders about legislative priorities, and presents legislative seminars.

National Institutes of Health (NIH) Stem Cell Task Force

Science Policy and Planning Branch
National Institute on Deafness and Other
Communication Disorders, NIH, Bethesda, MD 20892
(301) 402-2313 • fax: (301) 402-2265
e-mail: stemcell@mail.nih.gov
website: http://stemcells.nih.gov/research/nihresearch/taskforce

The NIH Stem Cell Task Force was formed to strengthen human and material resources necessary to enable and accelerate the pace of stem cell research. The task force seeks the advice of scientific leaders about the challenges to moving the stem cell research agenda forward. The website of the Stem Cell Task Force provides basic information on stem cell science, promising lines of research, ethical issues, and policy.

National Right to Life Committee (NRLC)

512 10th St. NW, Washington, DC 20004
(202) 626-8800
e-mail: NRLC@nrlc.org
website: www.nrlc.org

The National Right to Life Committee, a federation of fifty state right-to-life affiliates and more than three thousand local chapters, is recognized as the flagship of the pro-life movement. NRLC works through legislation and education to protect human life from abortion, infanticide, assisted suicide, and euthanasia. The NRLC website includes information on human cloning and embryonic stem cell research.

Pew Forum on Religion and Public Life

1615 L St. NW, Suite 700, Washington, DC 20036-5610
(202) 419-4550 • fax: (202) 419-4559
website: www.pewforum.org

The Pew Research Center's Forum on Religion and Public Life seeks to promote understanding of issues at the intersection of religion and public affairs. The Pew Forum conducts surveys, demographic analyses, and other social science research on important aspects of religion and public life in the United States and around the world. It also provides a neutral venue for discussions of timely issues through roundtables and briefings. The organization's website includes a page on religion and stem cell research.

US Conference of Catholic Bishops (USCCB)

3211 Fourth St. NE, Washington, DC 20017
(202) 541-3000
website: www.usccb.org

The US Conference of Catholic Bishops is an assembly of the hierarchy of the Catholic Church in the United States and the US Virgin Islands. The organization's website includes a page of resources, "Stem Cell Research," that includes church documents and teachings, fact sheets, articles, and publications reflecting a Catholic perspective on stem cell research and public policy.

US Food and Drug Administration (FDA)

10903 New Hampshire Ave., Silver Spring, MD 20993
(888) 463-6332
website: www.fda.gov

The FDA is responsible for protecting public health by assuring the safety, efficacy, and security of human and veterinary drugs, biological products, medical devices, the nation's food supply, cosmetics, and products that emit radiation. Its website provides information about stem cells and the importance of ensuring the efficacy and safety of stem cell-based products.

Bibliography

Books

Terence D. Allen and Graham Cowling	*The Cell: A Very Short Introduction.* New York: Oxford University Press, 2011.
Michael Bellomo	*The Stem Cell Divide: The Facts, the Fiction, and the Fear Driving the Greatest Scientific, Political, and Religious Debate of Our Time.* New York: American Management Association, 2006.
Diana DeGette	*Sex, Science and Stem Cells: Inside the Right Wing Assault on Reason.* Guilford, CT: Lyons Press, 2008.
Donna Dickenson	*Body Shopping: The Economy Fuelled by Flesh and Blood.* Oxford, United Kingdom: Oneworld, 2008.
Cynthia Fox	*Cell of Cells: The Global Race to Capture and Control the Stem Cell.* New York: W.W. Norton & Co., 2007.
Leo Furcht and William R. Hoffman	*The Stem Cell Dilemma: Beacons of Hope or Harbingers of Doom?* New York: Arcade Publishing, 2008.
Robert P. George	*Embryo: A Defense of Human Life.* New York: Doubleday, 2008.
Louis M. Guenin	*The Morality of Embryo Use.* New York: Cambridge University Press, 2008.

C.L. Mummery   *Stem Cells: Scientific Facts and Fiction.* Boston, MA: Elsevier/Academic Press, 2011.

Alice Park   *The Stem Cell Hope: How Stem Cell Medicine Can Change Our Lives.* New York: Hudson Street Press, 2011.

S. Steven Potter *Designer Genes: A New Era in the Evolution of Man.* New York: Random House, 2010.

L. Wolpert   *How We Live and Why We Die: The Secret Lives of Cells.* New York: W.W. Norton & Co., 2009.

Periodicals and Internet Sources

Jessica Berman   "Study Identifies Stem Cells as Cancer Source," *Voice of America,* August 3, 2012.

CBSNews Politics "Obama Ends Stem Cell Research Ban," June 18, 2009. www.cbsnews .com.

John Farrell   "Stem Cells in the News and Yokohama," *Forbes,* June 15, 2012.

Henry Fountain   "Synthetic Windpipe Is Used to Replace Cancerous One," *New York Times,* January 12, 2012.

Drew Griffin   "Family Hangs Hope for Boy on Unproven Therapy in India," *CNN Health,* May 21, 2012. www.cnn.com /health.

Kate Kelland   "Researchers Urge EU Not to Cut
                      Stem Cell Funding," *Reuters*, June 15,
                      2012. www.reuters.com.

Vanessa McMains   "Brain's Stem Cells 'Eavesdrop' to
                      Find Out When to Act," *EurekAlert!*
                      (Johns Hopkins Medical
                      Institutions), August 6, 2012.
                      www.eurekalert.org.

*Medical News   "A Link Between Stem Cell
Today*   Regulation and Cancer," August 7,
                      2012.

*Medical News   "In Animal Model, Heart Muscle Cell
Today*   Grafts Suppress Arrhythmias After
                      Heart Attacks," August 7, 2012.

Rosie Mestel and   "Stem Cell Findings Point Toward
Eryn Brown   New Cancer Treatments," *Los Angeles
                      Times*, August 1, 2012.

Andrew Pollack   "A Stem-Cell-Based Drug Gets
                      Approval in Canada," *New York
                      Times*, May 17, 2012.

Miguel   "On the Origin of the Term 'Stem
Ramalho-Santos   Cell'," *Cell Stem Cell*, June 7, 2007.
and Holger
Willenbring

Malcolm Ritter   "Stem Cells Could Fuel Cancer
                      Growth: Mouse Studies Support Idea
                      of Hidden 'Seeds' for Tumors," *ABC
                      News*, August 1, 2012.

Science Daily   "Bone Grown from Human
                      Embryonic Stem Cells," May 14,
                      2012.

Science Daily   "Mechanisms That Allow Embryonic Stem Cells to Become Any Cell in the Human Body Identified," July 18, 2012.

Science Daily   "Do Ovaries Continue to Produce Eggs During Adulthood?" July 26, 2012.

Science Daily   "Stem Cells Repair Hearts Early in Life, but Not in Adults," July 30, 2012

Jim Timmer   "Heart Tissue Derived from Embryonic Stem Cells Doesn't Skip a Beat," *Ars Technica*, August 7, 2012.

Gretchen Vogel   "Cancer Stem Cells Can Fuel Tumor Growth," *Wired Science*, August 2, 2012. www.wired.com/wiredscience.

Nicholas Wade   "Researchers Find Stem Cells Can Generate Human Eggs," *New York Times*, February 27, 2012.

Irving Weissman "Stem Cell Therapies Could Change Medicine . . . If They Get the Chance," *Cell Stem Cell*, June 14, 2012.

Index

CPSIA information can be obtained
at www.ICGtesting.com
Printed in the USA
FFOW050922290313
1047FF